MW00989917

AI Fundamentals for Business Leaders

Up to Date With Generative AI

Byte-Sized Learning AI
Book 1

I. Almeida

We are the most trusted and effective learning platform dedicated to empowering you with the knowledge and skills needed to harness the power of AI.

Contents

Part 7
Generative AI

Chapter 1

Navigating the AI Landscape: A Pragmatic Guide for Business Leaders

Today's business world is at a pivotal juncture, spurred by revolutionary technological advancements. Economic uncertainties and job losses exacerbate this complexity. As leaders grapple with balancing strategic cost reductions and smart investments, AI stands out as a promising pathway for decision-makers.

The allure of AI as an investment choice is indisputable. Its robustness, tested and proven across predictive models, has shown remarkable returns. This trust in AI's potential is reflected in Forrester's predictions, which see AI expenditure growing from $33 billion in 2021 to an astounding $64 billion by 2025. The impressive spending growth doesn't eliminate the high complexity and risk involved in AI application and adoption.

Moving beyond the proven AI capabilities, we encounter the enigmatic domain of Generative AI (Gen AI). This realm, characterized by tremendous hype, speculation, and potential disruptions, demands keen attention. Gen AI includes machine learning models like ChatGPT, Midjourney, Bing AI, Bard, and DALL-E. Trained on massive volumes of text and image data, these models generate new text and images in response to prompts, spurring innovation.

Understanding the Hype Cycle

With emerging technologies' noise and buzz, business leaders face a dilemma. There is the risk of missing out on groundbreaking opportunities offered by these technologies, but also the threat of mis-allocating resources on over-hyped technologies that cannot deliver on their promises. Navigating this complexity requires an understanding of the typical cycles of technology adoption: the hype cycle.

The hype cycle charts the life of technologies from inception to widespread adoption. An initial phase of inflated expectations, where success stories may be overstated, often follows the early enthusiasm. This phase can distort the perception of the technology's immediate capabilities and impact, creating unrealistic expectations. Businesses must accurately assess where a technology is within its hype cycle and adjust their adoption strategies, aiming for a balance between seizing promising opportunities and addressing practical needs.

Gen AI exhibits vast potential; however, as it currently sits at the peak of the hype cycle, businesses should maintain a balanced perspective. Its capabilities are still under development, despite early experiments showing its potential for innovation in content creation, design, and scientific discovery.

For example, exaggerated expectations around Gen AI can lead to the assumption that it can entirely replace human creativity. This narrative appears in sectors like digital art, music, and literature, where anticipation of AI replacing human creatives is high. However, while Gen AI can produce impressive content, it falls short in replicating the emotional depth, cultural nuances, originality, and personal experiences that human creators bring to their work.

Generative AI: Unleashing Real Value

Despite the exaggerated narratives, some sectors are recognizing how Gen AI can deliver real value. The technology is poised to bring significant transformations to various sectors, such as IT, marketing and sales, customer service, and product development.

- In the IT sector, Gen AI can augment teams by helping write code and documentation, potentially boosting developer productivity.
- In marketing and sales, Gen AI allows for the creation of automated ad campaigns, personalized customer interactions, and even

fresh product descriptions that can boost engagement and sales.

- In customer service, AI chatbots can answer queries, troubleshoot problems, and improve service response times.
- In product development, Gen AI can aid in ideation, design, and prototyping, fast-tracking innovation.

In the short term, some sectors are particularly well placed to capitalize on these applications. The media and entertainment industry can use Gen AI to produce unique content, brainstorm new ideas, and streamline the localization of IP, reducing the need for time-consuming human translation. Similarly, industries such as banking, consumer goods, telecommunications, life sciences, and technology stand to gain significant operational benefits, given their substantial investments in IT, customer service, marketing and sales, and product development. This underscores the widespread and transformative potential of Gen AI across a broad range of industries.

Challenges and Risks: Addressing the Other Side of the Coin

As much as Gen AI holds vast potential, it's also crucial to recognize and address the challenges and risks it presents. Misuse of the technology is one significant concern. GenAI can produce deepfakes and fake news, potentially fueling disinformation campaigns and damaging reputations. Data privacy issues also arise as these systems need large amounts of data for training, with the potential to expose sensitive information inadvertently.

A case in point is OpenAI's ChatGPT, known for its inaccuracies, which can harm a company's reputation if improperly used in customer-facing roles. Additionally, there's the risk of unintentional exposure of sensitive corporate data, as witnessed in companies like Samsung, which have issued cautionary advisories against using ChatGPT and similar AI services. Other organizations, such as JPMorgan and Amazon, have reportedly followed suit.

There's also the issue of job displacement. Though the goal is to have Gen AI augment human capabilities and not replace them, it's likely that jobs may be lost in the short term, especially in areas like content generation and customer service. Leaders need to balance the benefits of Gen AI adoption with the potential social and ethical implications.

Furthermore, although we still have scarce data on the carbon footprint of a single Gen AI query, some industry figures estimate it to be four to five times higher than that of a search engine query.

Evolving Value Chain and Commoditization of AI Tools

The Gen AI value chain is developing rapidly. This includes hardware, cloud platforms, foundation models, model hubs and machine learning operations (MLOps), applications, and services. Large tech companies currently dominate most of these areas.

Applications built on foundation models, which are fine-tuned for specific tasks, offer the highest potential for value creation. These applications can revolutionize various business functions and industries, including IT, marketing and sales, customer service, and product development. In turn, new services are emerging to help businesses navigate and exploit the opportunities offered by Gen AI.

As AI capabilities become increasingly commoditized, the value shifts towards data and domain expertise. It's no longer just about having access to AI tools and algorithms, but about the ability to curate high-quality, relevant data and the expertise to apply AI effectively.

Navigating Generative AI Adoption

Strategically adopting Gen AI requires a balanced approach that combines enthusiasm for the technology's potential with a pragmatic evaluation of its current capabilities and risks. Businesses need to educate themselves on the technology, run pilot projects to understand its potential impact, and create contingency plans for potential misuse or ethical issues.

The adoption of Gen AI is a journey rather than a destination. To embark on a successful journey of AI integration, business leaders must lay the foundation with a solid understanding of the underlying principles and concepts. Fundamental knowledge of AI (and Gen AI) is crucial for making informed decisions and identifying appropriate use cases.

Our Approach

This book aims to provide a straightforward introduction to the theory and applications of AI, machine learning, deep learning, and its new evolution—generative AI. The primary aim is to equip readers with the foundational understanding that will allow you to explore AI (and Gen AI) strategy, transformation, and governance in subsequent books in our *Byte-sized Learning* series.

To deliver the best learning experience, we may simplify concepts in the earlier chapters in the book, until we have the opportunity to provide more in depth definitions and examples later on, therefore building your understanding one step at a time.

We ask questions at the end of each chapter to prompt readers to reflect on their knowledge and test their understanding. This is part of our tried-and-tested pedagogic design. You will find answers to these questions on our AI

Academy platform, where you can access complimentary online quizzes, engage in community discussions with other business leaders, and enroll in the full course aligned with the National micro-credentials framework. This accreditation serves as tangible proof of the knowledge and capabilities obtained while reading this book.

Once you sign up to the AI Academy, you will receive an invitation to join our forums and continue your learning journey.

With a commitment to continuous learning and critical thinking, businesses can position themselves for long-term growth and success in the era of AI-driven innovation.

Part 1

Introduction to Artificial Intelligence

Chapter 1
Innovate and Adapt, Faster!

A journey two decades into the past would reveal a landscape starkly different from today's digital reality. The profound evolution of technology and the internet has catalyzed transformation across various sectors. The rise and fall of certain businesses over these years offers a captivating narrative of adaptation, innovation, and obsolescence.

The Rise of Digital

Turn back the clock to the early 2000s, when music enthusiasts would seek the latest CDs, cassettes, or vinyl records at stores like Tower Records or Virgin Megastore. Fast-forward to the present day, where digital music platforms like Spotify, Apple Music, and Amazon Music dominate the scene, offering millions of songs accessible in an instant. This shift towards digital convenience rendered physical music outlets redundant, ultimately leading to their closure.

A similar transformation occurred in the realm of home entertainment. In its heyday, Blockbuster was the hub for movie and TV show rentals. However, streaming platforms like Netflix, Amazon Prime Video, and Disney+ drastically reshaped this industry. Blockbuster's inability to anticipate and adapt to this digital wave resulted in its eventual downfall.

Brick-and-mortar retailers such as Barnes & Noble, Toys "R" Us, and Sears, once drew crowds with their physical outlets. However, the emergence of e-commerce powerhouses like Amazon revolutionized the shopping landscape. While Barnes & Noble somewhat managed to balance its physical presence with an online offering, Toys "R" Us and Sears faced significant challenges, struggling to stay afloat in this new digital age.

In the realm of search engines and email services, Yahoo! was once a major player. However, a lack of innovation and complacency paved the way for new disruptors. Google, with its superior technology and user experience, quickly overtook Yahoo!, establishing itself as a dominant force in the digital world.

Traditional taxi services also underwent a seismic shift with the emergence of app-based ride-hailing services like Uber and Lyft. The convenience, affordability, and user-friendly experience these platforms offered left traditional taxi services scrambling to adapt or risk becoming relics of the past.

This whirlwind of digital evolution underscores the dramatic changes in industries, from music and home entertainment to retail, search engines, and transportation. The saga of Tower Records, Blockbuster, Sears, Yahoo!, and traditional taxi services serves as a potent reminder of the potential consequences of failing to evolve and innovate in the face of digital disruption.

Digital Acceleration

The COVID-19 crisis acted as a significant accelerant for digital adoption. According to a 2020 McKinsey Global Executive Survey, companies advanced their digital capabilities by three to four years in just a few months. Digital or digitally enabled products saw an astonishing leap of seven years.

As the crisis unfolded, consumers rapidly migrated to online channels, leading businesses to fast-track digital transformations in customer interactions and internal operations. Investments in data security and cloud migration grew exponentially. The technology-oriented changes implemented during the pandemic are likely to persist post-crisis, and companies that embraced digital technologies have observed twice the revenue growth compared to their peers.

In this context, the COVID-19 crisis served as a historical inflection point that emphasized the importance of continual adaptation, digital resilience, and innovation in the business world.

The Next Wave of Disruption

While the seismic shifts of the internet era have reshaped many industries, businesses must recognize that their past victories don't assure future relevance. The emergence of artificial intelligence, particularly Gen AI, heralds another wave of disruptions.

This innovative technology, a subset of AI, specializes in creating novel content, such as text, images, or music, by learning from existing data. It poses significant opportunities and challenges even to the giants of the internet age.

This is vividly illustrated by Microsoft's ambitious initiative to challenge Google Search by incorporating OpenAI's Gen AI technology into Bing. Alphabet, Google's parent company, has also developed its own AI chatbot called Bard, and Baidu has announced it will follow suit.

Gen AI could be a game changer for search, potentially upsetting the established competitive order. However, the outcome is still uncertain, and there are numerous factors to consider, such as monetization, the importance of the network effect, and the existing dominance of established players like Google.

The internet era fundamentally altered communication, information exchange, and business paradigms. However, the AI era promises even more profound transformations, with a focus on automation, data analysis, and machine learning. Gen AI, stands at the forefront of these transformations.

In the realm of customer service, traditional roles are steadily giving way to AI-powered chatbots and virtual assistants, offering more personalized and efficient support. Companies lagging in the adoption of such technologies risk losing ground to their competitors, who deliver superior customer experiences.

Similarly, AI-driven recommendation engines used by businesses like Amazon and Spotify tailor their services to individual customers, enhancing customer satisfaction and loyalty. Ignoring the transformative potential of these technologies could cause stagnation or even decline.

AI is also sparking revolutions in sectors that were previously thought to be impervious to automation, like art, music, literature, diagnosing diseases, developing new drugs, and customizing medical treatments. These developments emphasize the pressing need for conventional businesses to compete effectively with their AI-empowered rivals.

As we transition from the internet era into the AI era, businesses must brace themselves for another surge of rapid technological advancements, incorporating Gen AI and other emerging technologies into their strategic planning and operations. By nurturing a culture of continuous learning, innovation, and adaptation, businesses can navigate the challenges of the AI era and secure their place in the dynamic, technology-driven landscape of the future.

———

Test Your Knowledge

A. What characterizes the AI era, as compared to the internet era?

1. Decreased levels of connectivity and information exchange
2. Increased focus on automation, data analysis, and machine learning
3. Diminished role of technology in business strategy
4. Reduced importance of data security and cloud migration

B. What type of technology is replacing traditional customer service representatives in some industries?

1. Blockchain technology
2. Virtual reality
3. Chatbots and AI-powered virtual assistants
4. Augmented reality

C. In the context of AI disruption, why is it important for companies to foster a culture that embraces change and continuous learning?

1. To compete with companies from the internet era
2. To retain traditional business models
3. To resist the adoption of AI technologies
4. To adapt to the rapidly changing landscape and effectively harness the power of AI

D. Why is the AI era considered potentially more disruptive than the internet era?

1. Because AI cannot improve efficiency or effectiveness
2. Because AI is less integrated into daily life than the internet
3. Because AI has the potential to reshape industries at an even faster pace
4. Because AI technologies are harder to understand and adopt than internet technologies

Test your knowledge online.

Chapter 2

AI and the Transformation of the Global Business Landscape

In recent years, AI has asserted itself as an instrumental catalyst for innovation across a plethora of industries. Companies are leveraging AI technologies to amplify efficiency, curtail costs, and augment decision-making by automating monotonous tasks, analyzing extensive data, and generating predictive insights.

For instance, AI has been instrumental in healthcare, enabling breakthroughs in medical imaging, drug discovery, and personalized medicine. In finance, AI tools have ushered in a new era in risk assessment, fraud detection, and investment management. In the retail sector, AI solutions have revolutionized supply chain management, demand forecasting, and the overall customer experience. With AI persistently evolving and permeating various industries, it becomes increasingly critical for businesses to comprehend, adapt, and use AI technologies to maintain their competitive edge.

However, to stay ahead in the AI era, it's essential for businesses to stay updated with the latest AI advancements and assess how these technologies can be integrated into their operations. The accelerated pace of AI innovation can intimidate, making it challenging for business leaders to identify the most effective strategies for AI adoption and execution.

Unlocking AI's Potential for Business Growth

According to PwC's Global Artificial Intelligence Study, AI's potential contribution to the global economy by 2030 is projected to reach a staggering 15 trillion US dollars. Furthermore, McKinsey reports that the rate of AI adoption has more than doubled since 2017. Despite this, risk mitigation to foster digital trust has remained alarmingly consistent since 2019. Advances in Large Language Models and Gen AI suggest that adoption rates will speed up, potentially overlooking trust and risk factors.

Also, analysts and consulting firms have consistently highlighted the high failure rate of Machine Learning (ML) projects, from both a delivery and benefit realization perspective. A 2020 Global Executive Study and Research Project by BCG and MIT Sloan revealed that while a considerable number of companies invest in AI, only a small fraction can scale their AI initiatives and derive substantial business value. The study found that only 10 percent of companies

glean significant financial benefits from AI technologies.

Simultaneously, reports from Gartner, Venture Beat, IDC,
and Dimensional Research collectively show that the
failure rate of ML projects varies between 78 and 87
percent.

While business leaders should certainly consider AI and
motivate their teams to investigate opportunities for
growth and productivity, the adoption of a single AI solution like ChatGPT doesn't equate to a comprehensive
business strategy.

In the AI-powered business landscape, success depends
on a holistic approach to AI implementation. This
approach should encompass not only the identification
of AI opportunities but also the creation of a robust
strategy to tackle potential challenges and risks.

Indeed, many off-the-shelf AI applications already
outperform traditional manual processes and should be
part of a comprehensive AI strategy. However, deriving
profits from AI entails more than merely integrating a
black-box AI system and feeding it with vast amounts of
data. Business leaders must distinguish between the
hype surrounding AI and its actual capabilities and
potential for value creation.

Embarking on the journey to transform an entire organization towards an AI-centric model requires an extensive understanding of the technology and its potential
applications. The shift entails significant adjustments at

both the organizational and cultural levels within a company.

It's crucial for businesses to establish certain foundational elements to ease the integration of AI. These prerequisites include access to relevant data, the provision of a supportive technological infrastructure, and the assembly of a skilled workforce. It's worth highlighting that the required talent extends far beyond mere programming expertise. It also demands professionals who can effectively and ethically apply AI, interpret its results, integrate it with existing systems, and navigate the challenges of change management associated with AI integration. By thoroughly addressing these aspects, companies can position themselves favorably to harness the myriad benefits offered by AI technologies.

One challenge companies may face is the potential for early failures, leading to irrational retreats. We have seen this in the past with online divisions because of the internet, and it's likely to repeat itself with AI. Companies can avoid falling into this pattern by learning from the past and not retreating from AI too quickly.

An approach that carefully balances quick wins or 'low hanging fruit' with long-term strategic work on foundational elements yields the best results. Moreover, restricting experiments with risky emerging technology on low stakes use cases is also crucial.

However, such a balanced strategy can only be effective when leadership truly comprehends the basic principles of this disruptive technology. Leaders must understand not only what AI can do, but also how it can be effectively and responsibly implemented to provide real value. They must be prepared to invest in both immediate applications that can provide a rapid return on investment, and in the underlying infrastructure and skills development that will support more complex applications in the future. By grasping the fundamentals of AI, leaders can make informed decisions, fostering an environment that balances immediate advancements with enduring, strategic growth in the AI era.

Let's get started!

_____

Test Your Knowledge

A. What is required for a successful transformation towards an AI-centric business model?

1. Access to relevant data, a supportive technological infrastructure, and a skilled workforce.
2. Just a strong AI software.
3. Only a team of AI programmers.
4. No change in the organization's current systems.

B. What does a balanced AI implementation strategy entail?

1. Only focusing on immediate applications for quick wins.
2. Only focusing on long-term strategies and ignoring immediate opportunities.
3. Balancing quick wins with long-term strategic work on foundational elements.
4. Avoiding AI adoption due to high failure rates.

Test your knowledge online.

Chapter 3
What is Artificial Intelligence?

Artificial Intelligence (AI) is a rapidly growing field that focuses on getting computers to perform tasks that typically require human intelligence. In other words, it's all about teaching machines to do things that normally only humans can do.

Artificial Intelligence is the capability of a machine to imitate intelligent human behavior.

> — John McCarthy, one of the founders of the field of AI

AI encompasses a broad range of techniques, including machine learning, natural language processing, computer vision, and robotics, among others. These techniques enable computers to understand language, reason, recognize speech, make decisions, navigate the visual world, learn, and manipulate physical objects, among other capabilities.

So, how does AI actually work? At its core, AI is achieved through the development of algorithms and models that allow:

- computers to process and analyze large amounts of data,
- learn from that data,
- and use that learning to perform various tasks.

Machine Learning, in particular, is a key technique used in AI. It focuses on getting computers to learn from data without being explicitly programmed.

What's exciting about AI is the potential it has to revolutionize the way we live and work. From self-driving cars to intelligent personal assistants, the possibilities are endless.

The Next Wave of Transformation

Technology has transformed businesses over the past few decades, and AI is undoubtedly the next important phase of digital transformation.

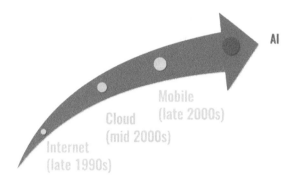

AI differs from traditional technologies as it has the potential to be a general-purpose technology that can be used in a wide range of sectors. As a general-purpose technology, AI has the potential to stimulate innovation and economic growth and inform product strategy and organizational design/strategy.

The signs are clear that AI is a general-purpose technology. It's being used widely across many industries, such as healthcare, finance, retail, and manufacturing. There is also a high volume of research jobs related to AI that are widespread across many industries.

As machine learning is a general-purpose technology, there are several implications for firms.

- Firms must realize that most industries are likely to change.
- They must be patient, as the transformative impact of AI may come with a lag.
- To effectively leverage the opportunities, managers need to understand the technology

and its applications and change their business models, technology infrastructure, organizational processes, and culture.

Managing Expectations

AI is an incredibly powerful tool that has the potential to transform many industries, but it's important to manage expectations about what it can and cannot do. A good rule for AI is to avoid being too optimistic or too pessimistic about its capabilities.

The sweet spot is to recognize that AI can't do everything, but it will transform industries. We need to embrace the possibilities of AI, but also be realistic about its limitations and risks.

Performance

One of the major limitations of AI is performance. While AI can be incredibly powerful, it's not perfect, and it can make mistakes. It's important to recognize that AI is only as good as the data it's trained on, and if the data is biased or flawed, the AI will be, too.

Explainability

Another challenge is the explainability of AI. Sometimes it's hard to understand why an AI system made a certain decision or took a certain action. However, researchers are working to make AI more explainable, and there are techniques like counterfactual analysis that can help us understand why an AI system made a particular decision.

Bias

Another risk associated with AI is biased AI. Biased data can lead to biased AI, which can perpetuate and even amplify existing biases in society. It's important to ensure that AI systems are trained on diverse and representative data to mitigate this risk.

Malicious Actors

Finally, there is the risk of misuse and adversarial attacks on AI. Malicious actors can use AI to create fake videos, manipulate data, and even create new threats that are difficult to detect. It's important to take steps to prevent these kinds of attacks, such as using security protocols and training AI systems to recognize and reject adversarial inputs.

Managing expectations about what AI can and cannot do is critical to realizing its potential. We need to strike a balance between optimism and pessimism, recognizing the limitations and risks associated with the technology while embracing its transformative potential.

Subfields of AI

Artificial Intelligence (AI), Machine Learning (ML), Deep Learning (DL), and Generative AI (Gen AI) are four terms that are often used interchangeably, but they refer to different concepts.

1. **Artificial Intelligence** is a broad field that involves creating machines that can perform tasks that typically require human intelligence. AI encompasses a wide variety of techniques and approaches, including ML, DL, and Gen AI.

2. **Machine Learning** is a subfield of AI that focuses on creating algorithms and models that allow machines to learn from data without being explicitly programmed. In other words, ML involves training machines to recognize patterns in data and use those patterns to make predictions or decisions. ML algorithms can be supervised, unsupervised, or reinforcement-based, depending on the type of learning used.

3. **Deep Learning** is a subfield of ML that uses artificial neural networks (ANNs) to learn from large amounts of data. ANNs are modeled after the structure of the human brain and are capable of learning complex patterns in data. DL is often used for image and speech recognition, natural language processing, and other

tasks that require a deep understanding of complex data.

4. **Generative AI** is a subset of deep learning. It uses artificial neural networks to process both labeled and unlabeled data. Generative models can generate new data instances, while discriminative models discriminate between different data instances. In essence, Gen AI models learn patterns in content and generate new content based on those patterns. Gen AI can generate natural language, images, audio, and other types of content.

While these terms are related, they each refer to different techniques and approaches to machine intelligence. By combining these approaches, researchers can create more advanced and sophisticated AI systems that can tackle complex problems and learn from their environment.

Data is Critical

Data is critical for machine learning because machine learning algorithms rely on large amounts of data to identify patterns and make predictions. Machine learning models are essentially mathematical models that can be trained to recognize patterns in data and make predictions based on those patterns. The more data a machine learning model has access to, the better it can learn and make accurate predictions.

Deep learning models are particularly effective when there is a large amount of data available for training. This is because the more data the model has access to, the better it can learn and identify complex patterns in the data.

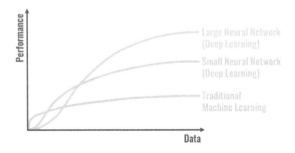

In contrast, traditional machine learning models often rely on handcrafted features that require expert knowledge to design and extract. This can be time-consuming, expensive, and limited in its ability to capture complex relationships in the data.

Test Your Knowledge

A. Which of the following statements about Artificial Intelligence (AI) is true?

1. AI only focuses on creating algorithms for specific tasks.
2. AI involves creating machines that can perform tasks typically requiring human intelligence.
3. AI is limited to natural language processing and computer vision.
4. AI is only used in healthcare and finance industries.

B. What is the primary difference between Artificial Intelligence, Machine Learning, and Deep Learning?

1. AI is a subfield of ML, and DL is a subfield of AI.
2. AI, ML, and DL are interchangeable terms.
3. AI is a broad field, ML is a subfield of AI, and DL is a subfield of ML.
4. ML and DL are unrelated to AI.

C. Which of the following is a challenge associated with implementing AI effectively?

1. AI has limited applications in various industries.
2. AI doesn't require any investment in technology and talent.
3. AI can lead to privacy, ethics, and bias concerns.
4. AI has no impact on workforce transition.

D. Why is data critical for machine learning?

1. Data isn't important for machine learning algorithms.
2. Machine learning algorithms rely on large amounts of data to identify patterns and make predictions.
3. Machine learning algorithms perform better with smaller amounts of data.
4. Data is only important for deep learning, not for machine learning.

Test your knowledge online.

Chapter 4

Human Intelligence Versus Machine Artificial Intelligence

The idea that AI is approaching human-level intelligence is prevalent in much of today's discussions in academia, industry, and media. However, the two forms of intelligence still differ significantly:

- **Context Understanding**: While human intelligence excels at understanding and interpreting context based on past experiences, emotions, and cultural nuances, machine intelligence often struggles in this area. AI systems traditionally work in a rule-based context and rarely grasp the nuances of language, intent, or the unspoken elements of communication that humans naturally decipher.
- **Common Sense Reasoning**: Humans inherently have common sense that allows us to make assumptions or conclusions based on life experiences, even without explicit knowledge.

For instance, we understand that if a glass of water tips over, the water will spill out. Machine intelligence, however, lacks this ability. AI can only infer what it has been specifically programmed to understand or what it can learn from extensive data.

- **Learning Efficiency**: Humans can learn and generalize from a few examples or experiences, while machine intelligence often requires thousands or millions of examples to learn effectively. The machine learning process is fundamentally different and more data-intensive compared to human learning.

- **Emotional Intelligence**: Humans have emotional intelligence, meaning they can understand and empathize with the emotions of others. This enables complex social interactions. Machines, on the other hand, can at best simulate emotional intelligence based on programmed responses or learned patterns, but don't experience emotions.

- **Creativity and Innovation**: Humans can think abstractly, imagine new ideas, and be innovative, often leading to unpredictable bursts of creativity. Machine intelligence, while able to generate novel combinations of known elements, doesn't truly innovate or create in the same way because it lacks the capacity to think beyond its programming or learned data.

These differences underline that while machine intelligence can mimic and assist human intelligence in many ways, it doesn't replicate the breadth and depth of human cognitive abilities.

Let's dive deeper into a few areas to unpack some of the nuances of machine versus human intelligence, and try to make sense of the present moment.

Context

Understanding context is a significant factor in human communication and decision-making. We constantly apply both explicit and implicit context in our interactions and choices, deriving meaning and direction from the surrounding circumstances. These contexts influence our interpretation of the world, shaping our actions and responses. However, providing context, particularly implicit context, to AI presents a significant challenge.

Let's begin by differentiating between explicit and implicit context. Explicit context is forthright, often directly articulated or discernible. It covers the lucid, factual elements of a scenario that are simple to express and understand. For instance, if someone says, "The meeting is at 2 PM," the explicit context here is the timing of the meeting.

Conversely, implicit context is composed of unvoiced presuppositions, societal standards, emotional signals, and underpinning implications that are comprehended without being directly conveyed. For example, if someone remarks, "I could really use a vacation," the explicit context is the person's desire for a holiday. However, the implicit context might infer that they are feeling stressed or overworked and need a break.

While AI has made significant strides in processing and understanding explicit context, it struggles with implicit context. AI systems typically rely on algorithms and data to make sense of the world. They excel at analyzing vast quantities of data, identifying patterns, making predictions, and executing tasks based on this information. This data-driven approach makes them incredibly effective at handling explicit context.

However, when it comes to implicit context, the challenges multiply. Implicit context is often nuanced, relying heavily on intuition, cultural knowledge, personal history, and other complex aspects of human cognition. Given their computational nature, AI systems find it difficult to grasp these subtleties. This is a crucial limitation as the inability to understand implicit context can lead to misunderstandings, incorrect assumptions, and potentially inappropriate decisions or responses.

AI systems, lacking the necessary contextual understanding, have made mistakes. Here are some examples:

1. Machine translation systems sometimes make mistakes because they don't fully understand the context in which words are used. For instance, they can translate individual words accurately but may struggle with idioms, metaphors, or cultural references that require context beyond the literal meanings of words.

2. Autonomous vehicles have trouble navigating in complex traffic situations. Despite advanced sensors and predictive algorithms, these vehicles sometimes misinterpret situations due to their inability to understand the nuanced "social" rules of driving, such as interpreting the intentions of human drivers or pedestrians.

3. AI-based diagnostic or treatment recommendation systems make errors because they can't consider the whole context of the patient's condition. They miss nuances that a human doctor, understanding the patient's complete medical history and personal circumstances, would catch.

4. Personalized recommendation systems sometimes recommend irrelevant or inappropriate content, misunderstanding the user's preferences. For example, just because a user watched a horror movie doesn't mean they want to watch all horror movies.

5. AI content moderation systems have mistakenly flagged or removed content that didn't violate platform rules. This usually happens because these AI systems lack the contextual understanding to interpret the difference between offensive content and content that's merely discussing or condemning the offensive behavior.

6. Despite its proficiency in understanding the grammar and vocabulary, natural language processing systems often misinterpret the sentiment or fail to grasp sarcasm, humor, or irony, leading to miscommunication or misunderstanding.

These examples collectively underline that while AI has become increasingly sophisticated, its understanding of context remains a significant challenge. This lack of contextual understanding is a limiting factor in the effectiveness and accuracy of AI systems, reinforcing the importance of continued human involvement in their deployment and oversight.

Moreover, sophisticated adversaries might exploit an AI system's lack of contextual understanding to manipulate its behavior or decision-making processes. This highlights the need for robust security measures and continuous monitoring to ensure the integrity of AI systems.

True intelligence is not just about processing information and executing tasks; it also involves the ability to understand and interpret the world accurately, incorporating past experiences and emotional understanding. At present, AI systems are primarily data-driven, focusing on pattern recognition and predictive analysis. Integrating the deeper aspects of understanding and interpretation, particularly relating to implicit context, is an ongoing challenge.

As we move forward, it's crucial to continue exploring methods to imbue AI with a deeper understanding of the context, thereby bringing it closer to true intelligence. In the meantime, keeping humans in the driving seat literally and figuratively is crucially important.

AI's Role in Creativity

AI has transformed multiple sectors, revolutionizing processes and introducing efficiency in unprecedented ways. A particularly interesting sphere where AI has made significant strides is in the realm of creativity.

The power of AI lies in its ability to analyze vast amounts of data, recognize patterns, and make predictions based on these patterns. When applied to the realm of creativity, these capabilities have the potential to unlock new avenues of expression and innovation. From generating music and visual arts to aiding in writing and design, AI tools are being used to augment human creativity in various ways.

Currently, millions of people are already using AI to create new content. Utilizing tools like OpenAI's GPT series or Midjourney, humans feed the AI inputs, and the model generates creative outputs. As the interaction between humans and the AI deepens, an intriguing consequence emerges - the humans often lose track of the origin of the creative output, blurring the line between human and artificial creativity.

This loss of distinction isn't necessarily a negative outcome. On the contrary, it signifies the successful integration of AI as a tool for creative expression. As the AI model mirrors and generates creative content, it becomes an extension of the human's creative process. Over time, the AI model could become as indispensable as any other creative tool, highlighting the symbiotic relationship between humans and AI in the creative process.

However, this relationship between AI and human creativity also throws up several philosophical and ethical questions. At what point does the creative output become solely that of the AI, and what does this mean for concepts like authorship and originality? Moreover, as AI becomes more integral to our creative processes, how do we ensure that the human element isn't lost?

Also, as we interact with AI, especially in creative endeavors, we often ascribe human-like attributes to it. We view AI not just as a tool, but as a collaborator, attributing creativity to the AI itself. This projection, called anthropomorphism, hints at our deep-seated need to humanize our tools and surroundings, bringing a psychological dimension to the interaction between humans and AI.

Yet, it's crucial to remember that AI, no matter how advanced, doesn't possess creativity in the human sense. It doesn't have experiences, emotions, or an under-standing of context - all elements that form the bedrock of human creativity. AI is a tool that can generate fasci-nating results based on its programming and inputs, but the direction, intent, and ultimate responsibility for the creative process still rest with the human.

Despite these philosophical debates, there's no denying that AI holds significant potential in the realm of creativ-ity. As we continue to explore this potential, it's essential to maintain a balanced perspective. Leveraging AI for creative purposes should not result in the abdication of human involvement or responsibility. Instead, the goal should be to foster a synergistic relationship, where AI augments human creativity, sparking new ideas and possibilities.

While AI offers intriguing possibilities, it also challenges our understanding of creativity and our relationship with our creations. As we continue this journey, it's clear that the exploration of AI's role in creativity is not just about technology, but also about understanding ourselves better.

Thinking, Fast and Slow Comparison

In understanding the nature and limitations of GPT assistants, such as OpenAI's GPT-4, OpenAI's Andrej Karpathy brings in the psychological concept of 'System 1' and 'System 2' as presented by Daniel Kahneman in his seminal book, "Thinking, Fast and Slow". System 1 represents our intuitive, automatic thought processes, such as recognizing a face in a crowd or understanding simple sentences. In contrast, System 2 corresponds to slower, more deliberate thinking, such as solving a complex math problem or critically evaluating an argument.

Karpathy likens Large Language Models (LLMs), like GPT-4 to System 1, highlighting their prowess in handling an extensive range of prompts, generating coherent text, and accomplishing tasks within their training data scope. However, much like System 1 in the human brain, LLMs can be susceptible to errors, especially when navigating complex or ambiguous tasks.

On the other hand, the characteristics of System 2—deep understanding, planning, reasoning—are yet to be fully realized in LLMs. Despite being capable of generating impressive outputs, LLMs do not truly understand the content they process or generate. They lack the ability to question, reflect, or reason in the way that human beings can with their System 2 thinking.

This comparison underscores the challenges that lie ahead in AI research while also providing a lens to appreciate the accomplishments so far. The aim is not to replace human thinking but to build systems that can supplement and enhance our System 2 abilities, creating a synergy between human intelligence and artificial intelligence.

———

Test Your Knowledge

A. Which of the following is a key difference between human intelligence and machine intelligence?

1. Human intelligence lacks common sense reasoning.
2. Machine intelligence can understand implicit context better than humans.
3. Human intelligence requires extensive data to learn effectively.

4. Machine intelligence can replicate the breadth and depth of human cognitive abilities.

B. Why is understanding the context important in human communication and decision-making?

1. It helps humans understand the explicit facts of a situation.
2. It allows humans to analyze vast quantities of data and make predictions.
3. It enables humans to navigate complex traffic situations.
4. It influences how humans interpret the world, shape their actions, and respond appropriately.

C. What is the difference between explicit and implicit context?

1. Explicit context refers to unspoken assumptions, while implicit context refers to observable facts.
2. Explicit context is easy to communicate and understand, while implicit context relies on intuition and personal history.
3. Explicit context is based on cultural norms, while implicit context is the factual aspect of a situation.
4. Explicit context can be derived from emotional cues, while implicit context is plainly stated or observable.

D. Which of the following is a challenge for AI systems in understanding implicit context?

1. AI systems excel at analyzing vast quantities of data.
2. AI systems struggle with interpreting the intentions of human drivers or pedestrians.
3. AI systems can understand idioms and metaphors accurately.
4. AI systems find it difficult to grasp nuanced aspects of human cognition.

E. Which of the following is an example of AI systems making mistakes due to their lack of contextual understanding?

1. Machine translation systems accurately translating idioms and metaphors.
2. Autonomous vehicles navigating complex traffic situations flawlessly.
3. Personalized recommendation systems recommending relevant content based on user preferences.
4. AI-based diagnostic systems considering the complete context of a patient's condition.

F. How does the phenomenon of anthropomorphism manifest in our interactions with AI, especially in the context of creative endeavors?

1. We view AI merely as a tool and do not attribute any human-like characteristics to it.
2. We ascribe human-like attributes to AI, often viewing it as a collaborator and attributing creativity to the AI itself.
3. We tend to ignore the role of AI and attribute all creative outcomes solely to human effort.
4. We view AI as a rival in the creative process, competing for the attribution of creativity.

G. What philosophical and ethical questions arise from the increasing role of AI in creative processes?

1. What will be the price of AI in the future, and who will have access to it?
2. How can we improve the efficiency and speed of AI in creative outputs?
3. At what point does the creative output become solely that of the AI, and what does this mean for concepts like authorship and originality?
4. How can we further humanize AI to make it more relatable?

Test your knowledge online.

Chapter 5

Key Applications

In this chapter, we'll outline some of the many applications of Artificial Intelligence to provide you with a sense of its broad applicability.

Natural Language Processing (NLP)

NLP, a significant facet of AI, aims at bridging the communication gap between computers and humans, enabling seamless interaction through natural language. The applications of NLP are deeply entrenched in our daily routines, powering voice assistants like Siri, aiding in text prediction for search engines, or even translating webpages into a variety of languages in real-time.

Prominent Applications of NLP:

- **Text Classification:** This application aids in filtering out spam emails and messages by categorizing them based on their content and context.

- **Sentiment Analysis:** NLP enables businesses to gauge customer satisfaction and identify areas of improvement by analyzing customer feedback on social media platforms.
- **Search:** Search engines leverage NLP to improve their search algorithms, providing more accurate and relevant results by analyzing the context and semantics of the queries.
- **Machine Translation:** NLP facilitates effective communication across borders by providing accurate translations between languages.
- **Text Generation:** News organizations leverage NLP to automate news article creation, enhancing journalism workflows.

Computer Vision

Computer vision, another key subfield of AI, equips machines with the ability to see and interpret visual data. This technology powers a wide array of applications, from facial recognition used to unlock smartphones to navigation systems in self-driving cars.

Key Applications of Computer Vision:

- **Image Classification:** AI models classify images into various categories based on their content.

- **Object Detection:** Security systems use object detection algorithms to identify suspicious activities in real-time.
- **Semantic Segmentation:** Self-driving cars use semantic segmentation to understand their surroundings and avoid obstacles.
- **Image Generation:** Game developers employ AI models to generate high-quality gaming environments.

Speech Recognition

Speech recognition technology, an integral part of AI, translates spoken language into written text. This technology powers virtual assistants, transcription services, voice biometric systems, and a multitude of hands-free computing applications.

Prominent Applications of Speech Recognition:

- **Automatic Speech Recognition (ASR):** ASR empowers voice-controlled devices and transcription services.
- **Text-to-Speech (TTS):** TTS converts text into natural-sounding speech, enhancing accessibility for visually impaired users.
- **Speaker Identification and Verification:** Security systems use speaker identification to authenticate individuals based on their unique voice characteristics.

Robotics

Robotics involves creating machines, known as robots, that can perform tasks autonomously. When combined with AI, robots can learn from their experiences, adapt to new situations, and carry out complex tasks.

AI-powered robots are found in many settings, from industrial assembly lines where they automate repetitive tasks, to hospitals where they assist in surgery. You might even have an AI-powered robot in your home, like a Roomba vacuum cleaner that learns the layout of your home for efficient cleaning.

Recommender Systems

Recommender systems use AI to predict and tailor content to user preferences. They're the reason your online shopping platform suggests products you might like or why your music streaming service seems to know your taste in music.

These systems have a significant impact on our online experience. They help us discover new products, books, movies, music, and even news articles that align with our interests, making the vast array of choices on the internet more manageable.

Anomaly Detection

Anomaly detection is the identification of rare events or observations which raise suspicions by differing significantly from the majority of the data. In the context of AI, this usually involves a system learning what 'normal' looks like and then identifying anything that deviates from that pattern.

For example, credit card companies use anomaly detection to identify potential fraudulent transactions. If you usually use your card in Texas and suddenly there's a purchase in London, the AI system flags this as anomalous behavior. Anomaly detection is also critical in areas like healthcare, where it can spot unusual patterns in patient data that may indicate a medical issue, and in IT security, where it can identify abnormal network traffic that may signal a cyber attack.

Bioinformatics

Bioinformatics is the application of AI and computational tools to understand and interpret biological data. As biological systems are exceedingly complex, AI has the potential to unlock new understanding in this field.

AI is used in bioinformatics to do things like predicting the 3D structure of proteins based on their amino acid sequences, identifying disease-associated genes, and analyzing medical images to detect diseases. It's also used to accelerate drug discovery by predicting how different drugs interact with targets in the body. With the aid of AI, researchers can analyze massive datasets quickly and accurately, potentially speeding up scientific discovery and the development of new treatments.

Healthcare AI Beyond Bioinformatics

AI is also used in other aspects of healthcare such as predicting disease outbreaks, improving patient care with personalized treatment plans, and administrative tasks like scheduling appointments.

Generative AI and Art

This includes applications like Midjourney and DALL-E, which can create art, music, and even write text based on user prompts. Gen AI models are also used to create realistic video game environments and special effects in movies.

AI in Agriculture

AI is being used for precision agriculture, where it can help optimize planting schedules, monitor crop health, and even automate irrigation and harvesting.

AI in Climate Modeling and Conservation

AI models are being developed to predict climate change patterns and their impact on biodiversity. They are also used in wildlife conservation efforts to track and monitor animal populations.

Autonomous Vehicles and Drones

Beyond just self-driving cars, AI is being used in the development of autonomous drones for tasks like package delivery, agricultural spraying, or disaster response.

AI in Supply Chain Management and Logistics

AI can optimize delivery routes, manage inventory, and predict demand patterns to streamline supply chains.

AI in Education

AI can personalize learning experiences based on the learning pace and style of individual students. It is also used to automate grading and provide real-time feedback.

Explainable AI (XAI)

This is an emerging field focused on making AI decision-making processes more transparent and understandable to humans.

AI for Cybersecurity

AI and machine learning can detect and prevent cyber-attacks by identifying patterns and anomalies in data traffic.

Emotion Recognition

AI algorithms are being trained to recognize human emotions based on cues from speech, facial expressions, and body language.

In conclusion, the ever-expanding applications of Artificial Intelligence underscore its profound impact across various domains. From everyday interactions through Natural Language Processing and the omnipresent influence of recommender systems to complex tasks in bioinformatics, agriculture, and autonomous navigation, AI is truly revolutionizing our lives. The advent of newer applications, such as Explainable AI, emotion recognition, and personalized learning experiences, further signifies AI's continuous evolution. These advancements provide a compelling narrative of the transformative potential AI holds, not just as a disruptive technology, but as a fundamental pillar reshaping our future.

————

Test Your Knowledge

A. What is Natural Language Processing (NLP)?

1. A subfield of AI dealing with image recognition
2. The part of AI that helps machines understand, interpret, and generate human language

3. The technology that translates spoken language into written text
4. A subfield of AI dealing with robotics

B. Which of the following is NOT an application of Natural Language Processing?

1. Text classification
2. Image generation
3. Machine translation
4. Sentiment analysis

C. Computer vision is a field of AI that enables machines to:

1. Understand and interpret visual data from the real world
2. Understand, interpret, and generate human language
3. Predict and tailor content to user preferences
4. Identify rare events or observations which raise suspicions by differing significantly from the majority of the data

D. Speech recognition technology is crucial for:

1. Automatic speech recognition (ASR)
2. Text-to-speech (TTS)
3. Speaker identification and verification
4. All of the above

E. Recommender systems use AI to:

1. Authenticate individuals based on their unique voice characteristics
2. Predict and tailor content to user preferences
3. Perform tasks autonomously
4. Understand and interpret biological data

F. Anomaly detection in the context of AI involves:

1. The identification of rare events or observations that deviate from the normal pattern
2. The application of AI to understand and interpret biological data
3. The technology that translates spoken language into written text
4. The part of AI that helps machines understand, interpret, and generate human language

G. Bioinformatics involves:

1. The identification of rare events or observations that deviate from the normal pattern
2. The application of AI and computational tools to understand and interpret biological data
3. The technology that translates spoken language into written text
4. The part of AI that helps machines understand, interpret, and generate human language

H. Which of the following isn't a subfield of Artificial Intelligence?

1. Natural Language Processing
2. Computer Vision
3. Bioinformatics
4. Quantum Computing

Test your knowledge online.

Chapter 6
Computational Power and GPUs

The deep learning boom is closely correlated with the significant advancements in computational power. A key driver of this increase in computational capabilities has been the development and widespread adoption of Graphics Processing Units (GPUs). GPUs are specialized electronic circuits designed to handle the computations required for rendering images, animations, and videos. However, their unique architecture has made them particularly well-suited for parallel processing tasks, which are commonly encountered in deep learning.

Deep learning algorithms, especially those employing neural networks, involve numerous matrix and vector operations that can be processed in parallel. In contrast to traditional Central Processing Units (CPUs) that have a limited number of cores, GPUs possess thousands of smaller cores. This architecture allows GPUs to process multiple computations simultaneously, significantly accelerating the training and inference of deep learning models.

This increase in computational power has fueled the rise of deep learning, as we can train more complex models with millions or even billions of parameters in a reasonable timeframe. The availability of powerful GPUs has enabled researchers and practitioners to experiment with larger and deeper neural networks, leading to state-of-the-art results in various fields such as natural language processing, computer vision, and speech recognition. In turn, these led to the acceleration of Gen AI.

Both OpenAI's ChatGPT and Midjourney were trained on 10,000 Nvidia GPUs each. Nvidia controls more than 90% of the data center GPU market, with AMD most of the rest.

In addition to GPUs, other specialized hardware, like Tensor Processing Units (TPUs) and Field-Programmable Gate Arrays (FPGAs), have been developed to further optimize deep learning workloads. These hardware advancements, coupled with algorithmic improvements and the growing availability of large datasets, have propelled the rapid expansion and success of deep learning across numerous domains.

———

Test Your Knowledge

What role have Graphics Processing Units (GPUs) played in the deep learning boom, and how has their architecture contributed to the acceleration of deep learning model training and inference?

1. GPUs have not contributed significantly to the deep learning boom.
2. GPUs have been vital in the deep learning boom due to their unique architecture, which allows for parallel processing tasks, thus accelerating the training and inference of deep learning models.
3. GPUs have played a role in the deep learning boom by increasing the size of datasets used in deep learning.
4. GPUs have contributed to the deep learning boom by optimizing traditional Central Processing Units (CPUs).

Test your knowledge online.

Part 2
All About Data

Chapter 7
Big Data

Big data is like teenage sex: everyone talks about it, nobody really knows how to do it, everyone thinks everyone else is doing it, so everyone claims they are doing it."

— Dan Ariely, Professor of Psychology and Behavioral Economics

Big data refers to the large, complex and diverse sets of data that are generated in today's digital age. These data sets are too big and too complex to be processed and analyzed by traditional data processing methods. Big data is an essential concept in today's technology-driven world, as it enables organizations to derive valuable insights from large amounts of data to make better decisions.

The history of big data can be traced back to the 1990s when the term was first coined by John Mashey, a computer scientist. At that time, big data referred to data sets that were too large to be managed by traditional databases. However, the term became more widely used in the 2000s, as the explosion of digital data from sources such as social media, e-commerce, and mobile devices made it clear that traditional data processing methods were no longer sufficient.

The rise of big data has been driven by several factors, including the proliferation of digital technologies, the growth of social media, and the increasing use of sensors and connected devices. The volume of data generated by these sources has grown exponentially, and it's estimated that over 2.5 quintillion bytes of data are generated every day.

To effectively manage and analyze big data, organizations must have the tools and technologies to handle the volume, velocity, variety, and veracity of data.

1. Volume

To manage and analyze these large data sets, new technologies and tools have emerged, including Hadoop, Spark, and NoSQL databases. These tools enable organizations to process and analyze large amounts of data quickly and efficiently, providing valuable insights and opportunities for innovation.

2. Variety

Data can come in many forms, including structured data (like a spreadsheet), unstructured data (like social media posts), and semi-structured data (like an email). In addition, data can come from a variety of sources, including sensors, devices, social media platforms, and more.

Structured data refers to data that is organized in a specific and predictable way. It follows a set of rules and has a clear and well-defined format, making it easy to search, sort, and analyze. An example of structured data is a spreadsheet, where each column has a specific heading and each row corresponds to a specific record or piece of information.

Square Footage	Price (in thousands of dollars)
800	100
1000	120
1200	145
1400	170
1600	190
1800	215
2000	240
2200	260
2400	285
2600	305

Structured data is often used in databases and other computer systems, where the data is organized and stored in a consistent and efficient way. It can be easily accessed and analyzed using tools like SQL, which is a language used to manage and analyze relational databases.

Structured data is useful because it allows for efficient searching, sorting, and analysis. It also makes it easy to compare data from different sources and to create reports and visualizations. The structure of the data set is an essential aspect of big data, as it determines how easily the data can be analyzed and used.

This type of data represents only a small percentage of the data handled by a typical organization.

Typical Organization's Data

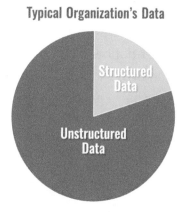

Unstructured data refers to data that isn't organized in a specific or predictable way. It doesn't follow a set of rules and has no clear and well-defined format, making it difficult to search, sort, and analyze. Examples of unstructured data include text files, social media posts, images, videos, and audio recordings.

Unstructured data can be challenging to work with because it requires more complex tools and techniques to search, sort, and analyze. Unlike structured data, there are no clear headings or fields to categorize the information. Instead, it requires tools like natural language processing and machine learning to extract insights from the data.

Despite the challenges, unstructured data is becoming increasingly important as more and more information is created. Social media, for example, generates vast amounts of unstructured data such as posts, comments, and messages. Analyzing this data can provide valuable insights into consumer behavior, sentiment, and trends.

Big data specialized tools and techniques, such as Hadoop and NoSQL databases, are designed to handle unstructured data and enable organizations to extract valuable insights from it.

Another way in which data varies is that it can take on many different forms and types, and understanding the nature of the data is essential for determining the most appropriate methods for analyzing it. Four common types of data are continuous, categorical, discrete, and time series.

- **Continuous data** refers to data that can take on any value within a certain range, like height and weight. Continuous data is often represented using a line or curve on a graph.
- **Categorical data** refers to data that falls into specific categories or groups, like gender, race, and occupation. Categorical data is often represented using bar charts or pie charts.
- **Discrete data** refers to data that can only take on specific values, like the number of children in

a family is a discrete data type because it can only take on specific integer values. Discrete data is often represented using histograms or frequency tables.

- **Time series data** refers to data that is collected over time at regular intervals, like stock prices, weather patterns, and sales figures. Time series data is often represented using line graphs or scatter plots.

Understanding the type of data is crucial for selecting the appropriate statistical methods and algorithms for analysis.

3. Velocity

The speed at which data is created is another important aspect of big data. Real-time data, such as data from sensors or social media, requires specialized tools and techniques to analyze in real-time. Streaming analytics, for example, can be used to analyze data as it's generated, enabling organizations to make decisions quickly based on real-time insights.

4. Veracity

Veracity refers to the quality and accuracy of data. With so much data being generated, it's important to ensure that the data is accurate, relevant, and trustworthy. Veracity is about ensuring that the data is reliable and free from errors, biases, and inconsistencies.

Data and Artificial Intelligence

A Machine Learning dataset is a collection of data used to train and test machine learning models. These datasets are carefully curated to include a variety of examples that represent the problem the model is trying to solve. ML datasets can come in many different forms, including text, images, videos, and numerical data.

	Inputs = Features		Outputs = Targets
Location	**Number of Bedrooms**	**Square metres**	**Price**
Balmain	1	55	1m
Newton	2	70	1.4m
Glebe	4	100	3m

For example, a dataset of images might be used to train a computer vision model to recognize cats and dogs. The dataset would include thousands of images, with labels indicating if a dog is in each image. Similarly, a dataset of text might be used to train a natural language processing model to perform sentiment analysis on customer reviews. The dataset would include thousands of customer reviews, each labeled with a sentiment score indicating whether the review is positive, negative, or neutral.

However, data doesn't always come cleaned and structured.

Feature Engineering

Inputs   Outputs

Feature engineering is the process of selecting and transforming raw data features into a set of features that can be used as input to a machine learning algorithm. The quality and relevance of the features are crucial to the performance of the model, and feature engineering plays a critical role in building effective machine learning models.

For example, consider a dataset of housing prices with features such as the number of bedrooms, the size of the house, and the location. Feature engineering can involve transforming these raw features into more informative and relevant features, such as the ratio of the number of bedrooms to the size of the house, the distance to the nearest transportation hub, or the average price of houses in the same neighborhood. These new features can help the machine learning algorithm better capture the underlying patterns and relationships in the data and improve the accuracy of the model's predictions.

Feature engineering is a crucial step in building effective machine learning models, and it requires a deep understanding of the data and the problem at hand. The process can be time-consuming and iterative, involving multiple rounds of experimentation and evaluation to identify the most effective features for the model.

It can be as much an art as a science because it requires domain expertise and a deep understanding of the data being analyzed. The process involves selecting and transforming variables from the raw data that are most relevant to the problem at hand. This requires a combination of creativity, intuition, and analytical skills.

———

Test Your Knowledge

A. What are the four V's of big data?

1. Volume, Variety, Velocity, Veracity
2. Volume, Versatility, Velocity, Veracity
3. Volume, Variety, Validation, Veracity
4. Volume, Variety, Velocity, Verification

B. Which of the following tools is commonly used to process and analyze large amounts of data quickly and efficiently?

1. Microsoft Excel
2. SQL
3. Hadoop
4. Adobe Photoshop

C. Which of the following types of data is NOT considered structured data?

1. Spreadsheet

2. Social media post
3. Relational database
4. CSV file

D. In the context of big data, what does feature engineering involve?

1. Selecting the best machine learning model
2. Selecting and transforming raw data features
3. Cleaning data from errors and inconsistencies
4. Visualizing data to identify patterns

Test your knowledge online.

Chapter 8
Data Science Versus Machine Learning

Machine learning and data science are two distinct yet closely related fields that often overlap in their methods and applications. While both involve working with large amounts of data, there are fundamental differences in their approach, scope, and end goals.

In simple terms, ML is the ability of machines to learn without being explicitly programmed, while Data Science is an interdisciplinary field that uses scientific methods, processes, algorithms, and systems to extract knowledge and insights from structured and unstructured data.

Data science integrates various fields, including mathematics, statistics, computer science, and domain expertise. It's not limited to only statistical or machine learning methods but can include other computational and inferential frameworks.

A crucial aspect of data science is the ability to **formulate the right questions and identify relevant problems that can be solved using data.** While machine learning may be a tool used in this process, data science also requires a broad understanding of the data's context, including the domain from which the data is drawn and the implications of the findings.

A data scientist's role includes data cleaning, exploratory data analysis, statistical inference, and communication of results. They use their understanding of the data and the problem at hand to select the most appropriate modeling approach, which might be machine learning but could also include simpler statistical models or even deterministic models based on domain knowledge.

The role of a data scientist is often broader than that of a machine learning engineer. A data scientist is likely to be involved in every step of the data analysis process, from understanding the business problem, collecting and cleaning data, exploring and visualizing data, building and validating predictive models, to communicating results and insights to stakeholders. On the other hand, a machine learning engineer's primary focus is on designing, developing, and deploying machine learning algorithms.

———

Test Your Knowledge

A. Which of the following is NOT a role of a data scientist?

1. Data cleaning
2. Designing, developing, and deploying machine learning algorithms
3. Exploratory data analysis
4. Statistical inference

B. Which field involves formulating the right questions and identifying relevant problems that can be solved using data?

1. Machine Learning
2. Data Science
3. Both
4. Neither

C. Which of these tasks is more likely to be performed by a machine learning engineer than a data scientist?

1. Understanding the business problem
2. Designing and developing machine learning algorithms
3. Exploring and visualizing data
4. Communicating results and insights to stakeholders

D. What is Data Science?

1. The ability of machines to learn without being explicitly programmed
2. An interdisciplinary field that uses scientific methods to extract knowledge from data
3. A field limited to only statistical methods
4. The process of communicating results and insights to stakeholders

Test your knowledge online.

Chapter 9

Harnessing Data for Machine Learning: Strategies and Challenges

The success of machine learning algorithms largely depends on acquiring relevant, high-quality training data. The predictive accuracy of the models is dictated by the data's quality, volume, and relevance. In the next few chapters we delve into the strategies for acquiring and utilizing training data.

Mining Value from Archival and Historical Data

Many organizations amass significant reserves of archival or historical data over their operational years. This stored data presents an excellent opportunity to mine valuable insights and can serve as training data for machine learning models.

For example, a dataset comprising past hiring decisions can become a valuable asset for a machine learning model designed for resume screening. However, it's crucial to be vigilant about any biases that might have been prevalent in historical decisions, as these biases, when unchecked, can seep into the machine learning models, distorting their predictions and propagating unfairness.

Leveraging Human Data Labeling and Crowdsourcing

Labeling massive datasets is an often daunting challenge in machine learning, particularly when the labeling needs to be precise. Human data labeling comes to the rescue in these scenarios, where human intelligence meticulously classifies and annotates the data. The advent of crowdsourcing platforms has democratized this process, allowing organizations to distribute the data labeling task to a vast network of individuals, facilitating the generation of large-scale, accurately labeled datasets.

However, it's vital to address the concerns raised by the data labeling community in light of studies touting the supremacy of AI in certain data labeling tasks. While it's true that AI has shown considerable capabilities in classifying and annotating specific types of data, it's important to note that these technologies don't operate in isolation. They are trained, refined, and overseen by human operators who ensure the results aren't only accurate but also relevant and contextually appropriate.

Capitalizing on User Inputs and Customer Data

User-generated data offers a treasure trove of information for training data. Form submissions, votes, ratings, and user actions such as clicks and purchases provide real-time insights into user behavior and preferences. This data can be invaluable for personalizing user experiences or predicting future user actions.

Tools such as ChatGPT can harness these vast amounts of user input to improve its performance significantly. By interpreting and learning from the ways users interact with its interface, ChatGPT can gain insights into language nuances, user preferences, and other valuable information that helps it generate more accurate and contextually appropriate responses. In this way, the AI system leverages user inputs as a continuous source of training data, which helps it evolve and adapt to changing user needs and preferences over time.

However, the collection and use of user data come with substantial responsibility. Ensuring user privacy is paramount. Organizations must provide clear communication to users about what data is being collected, how it's being utilized, and how users can manage, correct, or delete their data. Techniques such as anonymization and data encryption can further fortify user data privacy.

Applying Advanced Techniques to Improve Data Quality

Advanced techniques, including data augmentation and synthetic data generation, can significantly enhance the quality of training data used in machine learning and AI algorithms, improving their effectiveness and utility.

1. **Data Augmentation**: This technique involves creating new data from the existing data set by applying various transformations that do not change the underlying meaning of the data. The goal is to make the model more robust by presenting it with diverse scenarios during training, thereby enabling it to generalize better when encountering unseen data.

For example, in the realm of image data, data augmentation techniques might involve rotation, scaling, flipping, or cropping the images. This helps the AI model to recognize the same object in different orientations, sizes, and positions, enhancing its ability to identify the object in new, unseen images.

For audio data, introducing noise or changing the pitch and speed of the audio clips can increase the model's ability to understand and transcribe speech even under less-than-ideal conditions. Text data can be augmented through techniques such as back translation (translating the text to another language and then back to the original language), synonym replacement, and sentence shuffling.

2. **Synthetic Data Generation**: Synthetic data is artificially created information that closely mimics real data. It is typically generated using various statistical methods, deep learning techniques, or simulation processes. One of the significant advantages of synthetic data is its utility in situations where the availability of real data is limited, either due to scarcity or privacy concerns.

For instance, in healthcare, privacy laws limit the use of patients' data for developing AI algorithms. Synthetic data, which mimics patient data but doesn't link back to any real individual, can be an effective solution. It allows developers to create, test, and train their models without infringing on privacy regulations.

Similarly, in autonomous vehicle development, real-world testing can be dangerous, time-consuming, and expensive. Here, synthetic data generated from detailed simulations of driving scenarios can be used to train and test self-driving algorithms more safely and efficiently.

Furthermore, synthetic data can be created to reflect specific scenarios or edge cases that may be underrepresented in the real data. This can help ensure the AI model performs well even in these less common situations.

While these techniques offer numerous benefits, it's important to note potential pitfalls. For example, data augmentation should be applied thoughtfully to avoid creating misleading data. Similarly, synthetic data must be generated carefully to ensure it faithfully represents the complexities of the real data. If used judiciously, these techniques can greatly enhance data quality and lead to more effective and robust AI models.

Addressing the Cold Start Problem

The 'cold start' problem is a common hurdle in data-driven fields, particularly in the realm of recommendation systems, where a lack of initial user data hampers the model's performance. To combat this issue, organizations can deploy a heuristic-based approach or include a calibration step to gather preliminary data. Another viable strategy involves developing hybrid models that combine the strength of collaborative filtering techniques, which rely on past user behavior, with content-based methods, which focus on the features of the items being recommended.

Let's consider a real-life example of a music streaming service like Spotify that employs a recommendation system to suggest songs and artists to its users.

When a new user signs up to the platform, Spotify initially lacks any data about their musical preferences - this is a classic example of a 'cold start' problem. The service doesn't yet know what kind of music the user likes, which artists they prefer, or which genres they typically avoid. This lack of data makes it challenging to deliver meaningful, personalized recommendations right off the bat.

To address this issue, Spotify might implement a heuristic-based approach in the initial stages. For example, during the user onboarding process, the platform might ask the user to select a few of their favorite artists, genres, or songs. This process helps the system gather some preliminary data about the user's preferences.

Alternatively, Spotify could employ a calibration step by recommending widely popular songs across various genres in the beginning and observing the user's inter- action with these suggestions. By monitoring which songs the user listens to completely, which ones they skip, and which ones they add to their playlist, the system can start building an understanding of the user's taste.

Once the user starts interacting more with the platform— by listening to more songs, following artists, or creating playlists—Spotify starts gathering more data about the user. This data then feeds into a collaborative filtering model, where the system recommends songs based on the listening habits of other users with similar tastes. Simultaneously, a content-based model would focus on the characteristics of the songs the user has enjoyed and recommend songs with similar features.

By using this hybrid approach, Spotify successfully navi- gates the 'cold start' problem and improves its recom- mendation system over time, creating a more personalized and engaging user experience.

Incorporating Feedback Loops

Feedback loops serve as a conduit for iterative improvement in many machine learning systems. These loops allow user interactions with the system's outputs to inform and refine the future outputs. Feedback loops can be explicit, soliciting direct feedback from users about the output quality, or implicit, deriving insights from user actions resulting from the model's output. While feedback loops can improve the model's performance over time and adapt to evolving data and new patterns, they need to be designed judiciously. Careless design could lead to self-reinforcing biases or echo chambers, where users only see content that reinforces their existing views or preferences.

Let's take YouTube's recommendation algorithm as an example to illustrate the implementation of feedback loops. YouTube's goal is to keep users engaged on the platform by providing them with content that they would find interesting and relevant.

Explicit feedback loops: When users interact with a video, YouTube offers them the opportunity to explicitly provide feedback. They can like or dislike a video, leave comments, or even report the video if it's inappropriate. This explicit feedback helps YouTube understand user preferences and refine its recommendation engine accordingly. For example, if a user frequently dislikes videos of a certain genre or from a certain channel, YouTube learns from this feedback and adjusts its algorithm to recommend fewer videos of that type to the user in the future.

Implicit feedback loops: YouTube also leverages implicit feedback from user interactions as a proxy for their interests and preferences. This includes user behaviors such as the length of time they spend watching a video, whether they skip it partway through, or if they share it with others. For example, if a user watches a lot of cooking tutorials, YouTube's algorithm picks up on this behavior and starts recommending more videos of that genre, even if the user never explicitly indicated an interest in cooking content.

However, while feedback loops are immensely valuable for personalization, they can sometimes inadvertently lead to echo chambers. For example, if a user watches a lot of videos from a specific political perspective, the recommendation system might continually serve more content that aligns with that perspective, potentially narrowing the diversity of information the user is exposed to. Therefore, it's crucial to design these feedback loops judiciously to balance personalization with the breadth of content.

Test Your Knowledge

A. What is one of the advantages of mining value from archival and historical data for machine learning models?

1. It is always unbiased.
2. It can serve as training data for machine learning models.
3. It requires minimal effort to collect and organize.
4. It is always current and up-to-date.

B. How does human data labeling support machine learning?

1. It ensures the data is always 100% accurate.
2. It allows for meticulous classification and annotation of data.
3. It eliminates the need for AI in data labeling tasks.
4. It guarantees that all data will be relevant to the model.

C. What are two methods to combat the 'cold start' problem in recommendation systems?

1. Heuristic-based approach and hybrid models.
2. Synthetic data generation and data augmentation.
3. Crowdsourcing and data encryption.
4. User inputs and historical data.

D. What is one of the main challenges when using user-generated data?

1. It is typically outdated.

2. It often contains biases.
3. It involves substantial responsibility for user privacy.
4. It does not provide real-time insights into user behavior.

E. How do data augmentation techniques improve the quality of training data?

1. By replacing the original data with new data.
2. By transforming the data in a way that does not change its underlying meaning.
3. By generating synthetic data that closely mimics real data.
4. By collecting more user inputs and customer data.

F. How does synthetic data generation assist in situations where real data is limited?

1. By creating artificial information that closely mimics real data.
2. By ensuring the data is always 100% accurate.
3. By increasing the quantity of real data available.
4. By replacing the need for real data entirely.

G. What are feedback loops in machine learning systems, and why are they important?

1. They are an ongoing source of user inputs.

2. They help to mine value from archival and historical data.
3. They allow user interactions to inform and refine future outputs.
4. They solve the 'cold start' problem in recommendation systems.

H. What is an example of an explicit feedback loop in YouTube's recommendation algorithm?

1. Monitoring the length of time users spend watching a video.
2. Users disliking a video or leaving comments.
3. Observing whether users skip a video partway through.
4. Tracking if users share a video with others.

I. What is a potential pitfall of feedback loops if not designed carefully?

1. They can be too time-consuming to implement.
2. They can lead to self-reinforcing biases or echo chambers.
3. They can always ensure 100% accuracy in machine learning models.
4. They can make the data augmentation process redundant.

J. In the Spotify example for addressing the 'cold start' problem, what are the two models that Spotify combines?

1. User feedback model and historical data model.
2. Collaborative filtering model and content-based model.
3. User interaction model and genre-based model.
4. Archival data model and user onboarding model.

Test your knowledge online.

Chapter 10
Proprietary Data as a Competitive Advantage

Data is the lifeblood of AI development. As demonstrated in previous chapters, machine learning algorithms, particularly deep learning models, require vast amounts of high-quality, diverse, and representative data to learn and refine their predictions or decisions effectively. The quality and uniqueness of the data that a company possesses can significantly impact the performance and success of its AI solutions.

Unique proprietary data sets can provide businesses with a competitive advantage in the AI era, as they offer the following benefits:

Enhanced performance: Access to unique, high-quality data sets enables companies to train and optimize their AI models more effectively, resulting in better performance, accuracy, and efficiency.

Differentiation: Companies that possess unique proprietary data sets can develop Vertical AI solutions that are tailored to their specific needs and requirements, setting them apart from competitors who rely on generic, publicly available data.

Barriers to entry: Unique proprietary data sets can serve as a moat for competitors, as they are more difficult to replicate or acquire. This can help companies maintain a competitive edge in their respective markets.

A great example of a company leveraging unique proprietary data sets is Tempus, a healthcare technology company that uses AI to analyze clinical and molecular data to improve patient outcomes in oncology. The company has built a vast proprietary data set of genomic, clinical, and imaging data from cancer patients, which it uses to train its AI models and develop personalized treatment plans. By leveraging this unique data set, Tempus has been able to create highly specialized AI solutions that cater to the specific needs of oncology patients, giving it a competitive advantage in the market.

However, challenges can arise quickly and change a company's competitive edge.

Stitch Fix, an online personal styling service, leverages AI and machine learning to offer personalized clothing recommendations to its customers. By accumulating a proprietary data set of customer preferences, feedback, and purchase history, Stitch Fix's AI algorithms can accurately learn and predict individual styles and preferences. This unique data set has allowed the company to stand out from competitors by providing a highly customized shopping experience.

However, Stitch Fix has recently faced challenges that led to a decline in active clients and net revenue per active client, resulting in a 1% revenue dip in fiscal 2022 and a further 21 percent decline in the first half of fiscal 2023. These struggles can be traced back to a difficult macroeconomic environment, tighter client budgets, and changes in Apple's privacy policy that affected the company's app's personal stylist features. Specifically, Apple's OS update permitted users to opt out of data tracking, which in turn disrupted the functionality of Stitch Fix's app and its ability to provide personalized styling services.

These obstacles underscore the significance of a well-thought-out and diverse data acquisition strategy in today's competitive landscape. Companies like Stitch Fix that rely on customer data to deliver personalized experiences must continuously adapt and evolve their data acquisition approaches to navigate changing regulations and external factors, ensuring that they maintain their competitive edge and continue to provide value to their customers.

————

Test Your Knowledge

A. Why is data considered the lifeblood of AI development?

1. Data helps in marketing AI products
2. Data is used to make AI models look appealing
3. Data is used to train and refine AI models effectively
4. Data is only necessary for deep learning models

B. What are the benefits of having unique proprietary data sets for businesses in the AI era? (Choose three)

1. Enhanced performance
2. Reduction in data storage costs
3. Differentiation
4. Barriers to entry
5. Increased simplicity

C. Why is it important for companies relying on customer data to continuously adapt and evolve their data acquisition strategies?

1. To navigate changing regulations and external factors
2. To reduce the overall cost of data storage
3. To make their AI models look more appealing
4. To eliminate the need for data in AI development

Test your knowledge online.

Chapter 11
Open Data and Data Sharing

While unique proprietary data sets can provide companies with a competitive advantage, open data and data sharing initiatives also play a crucial role in advancing AI research and development. Access to diverse, high-quality open data sets enables researchers and businesses to train AI models, test their performance, and iterate on their algorithms more effectively. This can lead to faster innovation and more robust AI solutions.

Open data initiatives can provide several benefits, including:

- **Democratizing AI**: Open data sets can lower barriers to entry for AI development, allowing smaller companies and individual researchers to access high-quality data and compete with larger organizations.

- **Fostering collaboration:** Data sharing initiatives can promote collaboration and knowledge sharing among researchers and organizations, accelerating the pace of innovation in AI.
- **Addressing societal challenges:** Open data sets can help researchers and businesses develop AI solutions that address pressing societal issues, such as climate change, healthcare, and poverty alleviation.

Several collaborative data sharing initiatives have emerged in recent years, aiming to foster innovation and advance AI research.

ImageNet is a large-scale, publicly available dataset of annotated images that has played a pivotal role in advancing computer vision research. The dataset, which contains millions of images labeled with thousands of object categories, has been widely used to train and test AI models for object recognition and classification. By providing a standardized benchmark for the AI research community, ImageNet has accelerated the development of computer vision technologies and contributed to the rapid progress in the field.

In response to the COVID-19 pandemic, the Allen Institute for AI, in collaboration with several research institutions, released the **COVID-19 Open Research Dataset (CORD-19)**, which contains tens of thousands of scholarly articles related to COVID-19 and other coronaviruses. The dataset aimed to facilitate research on the virus and support the development of AI-driven solutions for understanding, preventing, and treating the disease. By sharing this data openly, the initiative fostered global collaboration and accelerated the pace of innovation in the fight against the pandemic.

As these examples demonstrate, publicly available datasets can be a boon for organizations, particularly startups and academic researchers. These diverse datasets can offer a valuable starting point. However, it's crucial for users to understand the limitations and potential biases in these datasets.

Moreover, data sharing agreements can provide a way for organizations to leverage each other's resources to mutual benefit. These agreements should be managed carefully, with privacy, security, and ethical concerns in mind. Thus, a clear data sourcing strategy is essential for AI developers.

Tracking Data Provenance

In some instances, companies are using open-source datasets, like the LAION-5B, which contains billions of tagged images scraped from the web, including copyrighted works. Some developers offer artists the opportunity to opt-out from their works being used in the next iteration of the AI system. However, this approach often places the onus on content creators to protect their IP, which is far from ideal. Developers should consider ways to maintain the provenance of AI-generated content, increasing transparency and providing a valuable resource to counter potential infringement claims.

As the legal landscape around Gen AI rapidly evolves, companies must remain vigilant and proactive in protecting their interests. Striking a balance that respects the rights of original content creators while harnessing the potential of this groundbreaking technology is essential as Gen AI changes the nature of content creation.

Balancing Proprietary Data and Open Data initiatives

While both unique proprietary data sets and open data initiatives play crucial roles in the AI landscape, companies must strike a balance between protecting their competitive advantages and fostering innovation through data sharing. Businesses can navigate this delicate balance by:

Identifying core proprietary data: Companies should determine which data sets are essential to maintaining their competitive edge and focus on protecting and leveraging these assets. This may include data that is unique to their business, industry, or customers, and cannot be easily replicated or acquired by competitors.

Contributing to open data initiatives: Companies can participate in open data initiatives by sharing non-sensitive, non-proprietary data with the broader research community. This can help advance AI research and development, create goodwill within the industry, and potentially lead to new insights and opportunities for the company.

Establishing strategic partnerships: Companies can form strategic partnerships with other organizations, researchers, or institutions to collaborate on AI research and development. By pooling resources and sharing data in a controlled manner, businesses can drive innovation while still maintaining control over their proprietary data and intellectual property.

In conclusion, data is a critical component of AI development, and companies must carefully consider their data management strategies to compete effectively in the AI era. Unique proprietary data sets can provide a significant competitive advantage, while open data initiatives can foster collaboration and accelerate innovation across the AI landscape. By striking a balance between protecting their proprietary data and participating in data sharing initiatives, businesses can position themselves for success in the rapidly evolving AI market.

———

Test Your Knowledge

A. What is the role of open data and data sharing initiatives in AI research and development?

1. To provide companies with a competitive advantage
2. To limit access to high-quality data sets
3. To train AI models, test performance, and iterate on algorithms more effectively
4. To discourage collaboration among researchers

B. Which of the following are benefits of open data initiatives? (Choose three)

1. Democratizing AI
2. Reducing storage costs
3. Fostering collaboration
4. Addressing societal challenges
5. Limiting access to data

C. Which dataset played a pivotal role in advancing computer vision research?

1. CORD-19
2. ImageNet
3. Tempus
4. Stitch Fix

D. What was the purpose of the COVID-19 Open Research Dataset (CORD-19)?

1. To track the spread of the virus
2. To facilitate research on the virus and support AI-driven solutions for understanding, preventing, and treating the disease

3. To store personal information of COVID-19 patients
4. To predict the next pandemic

E. How can companies strike a balance between protecting their competitive advantages and fostering innovation through data sharing? (Choose three)

1. Identifying core proprietary data
2. Ignoring open data initiatives
3. Contributing to open data initiatives
4. Keeping all data private
5. Establishing strategic partnerships

F. Which of the following strategies is recommended for AI developers in regard to data sourcing and managing?

1. Leveraging only proprietary datasets for AI development to avoid copyright issues.
2. Ignoring the provenance of AI-generated content as it is not significant in the development process.
3. Utilizing data sharing agreements to benefit from mutual resources while carefully managing privacy, security, and ethical concerns.
4. Excluding open-source datasets in their AI development process.

Test your knowledge online.

Chapter 12

The New Era of Generative AI: Understanding the Data Management Implications

2023 has been a transformative year in the field of artificial intelligence, with Gen AI models like ChatGPT capturing widespread attention. These AI solutions hold significant potential for innovation and productivity. However, their limitations, especially around data privacy and data management, need wider comprehension.

Companies like Samsung have experienced issues with data leakage through AI services, while concerns about reliability, privacy, and security violations are continually rising. In response to these challenges, it's clear that regulations and standards need to be established for implementing AI technologies.

Unboxing the Black Box: Data Governance and Transparency

At the heart of these AI systems is the proprietary pre-trained AI model incorporating vast datasets from numerous sources, yet their transparency regarding this source data is minimal. As discussed in the last chapter, the lack of credibility, accuracy, and legality of the source data poses a significant issue. The potential for unverified or biased data being part of the model's training is alarming. Therefore, data governance requiring transparency in data sources used and the validity of knowledge from those sources is urgently needed.

Navigating Data Segregation and Domains

Data privacy is another critical concern. Different AI vendors follow varying policies regarding data privacy, leading to possible confusion and misuse. Companies run the risk of exposing sensitive data unknowingly. A possible solution lies in creating "domains" of data. Pre-trained AI tools should be able to segregate "general" training data and "proprietary data", ensuring the privacy of company-specific information.

Derivative Works of AI: Ownership and Accountability

Another aspect that needs attention is the data generated by the AI process itself. Questions surrounding ownership, accountability, and intellectual property arise when Gen AI tools are employed. Companies need to understand that they are liable for any errors resulting from tasks delegated to AI. Hence, clarity about IP ownership and its legal implications is crucial.

Implementing Data Management Tactics

1 **Recognizing AI Risks**: As AI technology is rapidly evolving, companies must be aware of potential risks related to data misuse, privacy violations, security breaches, and intellectual property infringements. A responsible approach requires organizations to mitigate these risks proactively.

2 **Governance Framework**: Establishing a governance framework can guide an organization's AI strategy, policies, and procedures. This can help to standardize AI use across the organization, ensure regulatory compliance, and provide mechanisms for mitigating risks.

3 **Data Management**: Implementing data management practices helps companies understand what data they have, where it's located, and how it's used. Such practices can improve data quality, support data privacy, and enhance the value derived from data. Limiting data shared with AI applications to only necessary information helps to keep sensitive and proprietary data secure.

4 **AI Tool Transparency**: It's crucial for AI tools to be transparent about their data sources and how they handle data privacy. Companies need to understand the data handling and privacy practices of the AI tools they use.

5 **Data Tagging**: Tagging data from derivative works can help keep track of data lineage and ownership. This can be beneficial in managing intellectual property rights and ensuring compliance with data privacy laws.

6 **Legal Consultation**: Legal consultation is crucial for companies to fully understand potential risks associated with AI projects. Legal experts can provide guidance on regulatory requirements, potential liabilities, and best practices for mitigating risks.

It's worth noting that while these tactics can help companies manage risks associated with AI, they're not exhaustive. The precise approach may vary depending on the specifics of the company's operations, industry regulations, and the nature of the data and AI applications in question.

AI technology promises significant advantages, from accelerating innovation and cutting costs to enhancing user experiences. However, it's important to navigate this terrain with caution. Clear standards for data management with AI are yet to be established. Until then, it's crucial for enterprises to understand the possible risks associated with data exposure, leakage, and security while using AI applications.

———

Test Your Knowledge

A. What problems have companies like Samsung faced in relation to AI services?

1. Data leakage
2. Lack of data
3. Excessive data

   4. Accurate data

B. Why is data governance in AI systems important?

   1. It makes AI models work faster
   2. It can prevent the use of unverified or biased data
   3. It is a legal requirement
   4. It makes AI systems cheaper

C. What solution is suggested to mitigate data privacy concerns with pre-trained AI tools?

   1. Segregating general training data and proprietary data
   2. Using encrypted data only
   3. Not using proprietary data at all
   4. Sharing all data openly for transparency

D. Who is liable for errors resulting from tasks delegated to AI?

   1. The AI model
   2. The company using the AI tool
   3. The AI vendor
   4. The individual who interacts with the AI tool

E. What should a governance framework for AI oversee?

   1. AI strategy, policies, and procedures

2. Only AI strategy
3. Only AI policies
4. Only AI procedures

Test your knowledge online.

Part 3
Machine Learning

Chapter 13
Business Leaders and Machine Learning

Business leaders must have some understanding of how machine learning algorithms work for several reasons:

Informed Decision-Making

Business leaders need to make strategic decisions about adopting machine learning technologies and integrating them into their organizations' workflows. By understanding the basics of machine learning algorithms, they can better evaluate the potential benefits, risks, and limitations of these technologies, and make more informed decisions on which algorithms or tools to use for specific business problems.

Effective Communication

Understanding machine learning algorithms enables business leaders to communicate more effectively with their data science teams, stakeholders, and customers. This knowledge allows them to ask relevant questions, provide appropriate guidance, and translate technical information into actionable insights for non-technical team members or clients.

Resource Allocation

Machine learning projects often involve significant investments in time, personnel, and infrastructure. Business leaders who understand the workings of machine learning algorithms can better allocate resources to projects that are likely to yield the most significant returns, ensuring that the organization's investments are optimally used.

Ethical Considerations

Machine learning algorithms can sometimes lead to biased or unfair outcomes because of the data used for training or the nature of the algorithms themselves. Business leaders with an understanding of these algorithms can proactively identify potential biases or ethical concerns and take appropriate measures to address them, promoting responsible AI usage within their organization.

Building Trust and Credibility

Demonstrating an understanding of machine learning algorithms can help build trust and credibility with employees, stakeholders, and customers. This is especially important when adopting new technologies or advocating for their use within the organization, as it shows that the business leader has a strong grasp of the potential benefits, risks, and limitations of the technology.

Staying Competitive

As machine learning and AI technologies become increasingly prevalent across industries, business leaders must stay informed about the latest developments and trends to remain competitive. Understanding the core principles and workings of machine learning algorithms enables them to stay ahead of the curve and identify new opportunities for growth, innovation, and efficiency.

Having a foundational understanding of machine learning algorithms is crucial for business leaders to make informed decisions, allocate resources effectively, communicate with technical and non-technical stakeholders, address ethical concerns, build trust and credibility, and maintain a competitive edge in an increasingly data-driven world.

———

Test Your Knowledge

A. Why is it essential for business leaders to understand the basics of machine learning algorithms?

1. To communicate more effectively with their data science teams.
2. To allocate resources more effectively.
3. To address ethical considerations related to machine learning.
4. All of the above.

B. Understanding machine learning algorithms isn't necessary for business leaders because they can always rely on their data science teams to make the right

1. True
2. False

C. How can understanding machine learning algorithms help in resource allocation?

1. It can help identify which projects are likely to yield the most significant returns.
2. It helps business leaders to identify the need for more staff.
3. It aids in the purchase of better machine learning software.
4. None of the above.

D. As machine learning and AI technologies become increasingly prevalent across industries, why is it necessary for business leaders to understand these technologies?

1. To stay competitive.
2. To increase the company's stock price.
3. To ensure their company is always in the news.
4. None of the above.

Test your knowledge online.

Chapter 14
Expert Systems

Before we define Machine Learning (ML), it's important to explain what are expert systems.

Expert systems, also known as knowledge-based systems, are a type of AI that is designed to simulate the decision-making abilities of a human expert in a specific domain. Expert Systems aren't ML, they are rule-based systems that use a knowledge base of domain-specific information and a set of inference rules to reason about new situations and make decisions.

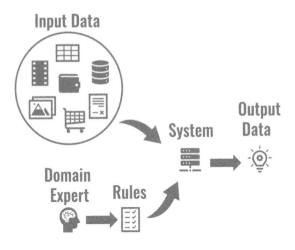

The approach of expert systems is to codify the knowledge of human experts in a specific field into a set of rules that can be used by a computer system to make decisions or solve problems. The knowledge base is constructed using a combination of human expertise and domain-specific data, and the rules are typically represented using if-then statements. For example, if the symptoms of a patient match a certain set of criteria, then a certain diagnosis or treatment plan may be recommended.

Advantages

One of the major advantages of expert systems is that they can provide consistent and reliable decision-making in a specific domain. They can also help to capture and preserve the knowledge of human experts, which can be valuable in situations where there is a shortage of experts or where experts aren't available at all times.

Another advantage of expert systems is that they can be used to automate complex decision-making processes, allowing organizations to save time and money while also reducing the risk of errors. For example, an expert system could be used to help diagnose medical conditions or to assist in financial decision-making.

Disadvantages

However, there are also some potential drawbacks to expert systems. One of the main challenges is that they can be expensive and time-consuming to develop, requiring significant resources to build and maintain the knowledge base and inference rules. There is also the risk that the rules may not accurately capture the full range of expertise and knowledge of human experts, leading to errors or inaccurate decisions.

According to Polanyi's Paradox, much of what we know isn't explicit or easily communicated, but rather resides in our personal experiences, intuition, and understanding of context. Tacit knowledge is often critical in decision-making and problem-solving and is difficult to transfer or formalize. As a result, expert systems may overlook or fail to account for important factors that a human expert would consider in making a decision.

For example, an expert system designed to diagnose medical conditions may be able to accurately identify and diagnose common diseases based on explicit rules and criteria. However, it may struggle to consider less common symptoms or take into account a patient's unique circumstances or medical history, which would be taken into account by a human expert.

Another potential disadvantage is that expert systems may not be able to adapt to new or unexpected situations, as they are limited by the knowledge base and rules that have been programmed into the system. This can make them less flexible than ML approaches.

Business leaders should review their expert systems and ask themselves which decision-making processes could be automated using ML.

———

Test Your Knowledge

A. What are expert systems, and what type of artificial intelligence do they represent?

1. Systems that employ human experts to make decisions
2. Rule-based systems that simulate human expert decision-making in a specific domain
3. Machine learning algorithms designed to learn from experience
4. Systems that rely solely on data to make decisions

B. What are the advantages of expert systems?

1. They can provide consistent and reliable decision-making in a specific domain
2. They can easily adapt to new or unexpected situations
3. They can capture and preserve the knowledge of human experts
4. They require minimal resources to build and maintain

Test your knowledge online.

Chapter 15
Machine Learning

While expert systems rely on the knowledge and rules encoded by human experts, ML involves using algorithms to automatically learn patterns and relationships in data.

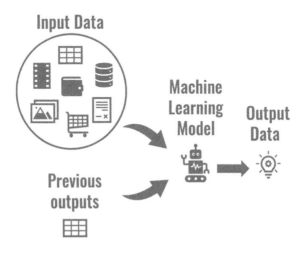

In ML, algorithms are trained on large amounts of data and learn to identify patterns and make predictions or decisions based on that data. The algorithms can adapt and improve over time as they are exposed to more data.

ML is increasingly being used in various fields, including e-commerce, cybersecurity, and finance. Three examples of how ML is used in practice are product recommendations, spam filters, and credit card fraud detection.

Product recommendations are a common feature on e-commerce websites. ML algorithms are used to analyze a customer's browsing and purchase history to recommend products that are relevant to their interests. For example, Amazon's product recommendation system uses a combination of collaborative filtering, which looks at what other customers with similar preferences have bought, and content-based filtering, which looks at the features of the product being recommended.

Spam filters are another area where ML has made a significant impact. ML algorithms are used to identify patterns in the characteristics of spam messages, such as the sender's address, subject line, and the content of the message. These patterns are used to train the spam filter to identify and block future spam messages.

Credit card fraud detection is another area where ML is used extensively. ML algorithms are used to analyze patterns in transaction data to identify suspicious activity. For example, if a card is used to make purchases in multiple locations within a short period, or if it's used to make purchases that are significantly different from the user's usual spending patterns, the system may flag the transaction as potentially fraudulent.

In all these examples, ML algorithms are trained on large amounts of data to identify patterns and make predictions or classifications. The algorithms learn from this data and become more accurate over time. This process is known as "training" the model. Once the model is trained, it can be used to make predictions or classifications on new, unseen data.

There are three main types of ML:

- Supervised Learning
- Unsupervised Learning
- Reinforcement Learning

Each type of ML has its own strengths and weaknesses, and is suited to different types of problems. Supervised learning is well-suited to problems where the target variable is known, while unsupervised learning is useful for finding patterns and structure in complex data sets. Reinforcement learning is ideal for problems where the optimal decision depends on the current state of the environment and the actions of other agents. We will cover this in detail in the following chapters.

ML has proven to be a valuable tool for businesses across various industries. It has enabled automation, accurate predictions, and personalized experiences for customers.

———

Test Your Knowledge

A. What is the key difference between expert systems and machine learning?

1. Expert systems are manual while machine learning is automated
2. Expert systems require human experts for rules and knowledge encoding, while machine learning uses algorithms to learn patterns in data
3. Expert systems are outdated while machine learning is the new standard
4. There is no difference

B. What does it mean to "train" a machine learning model?

1. It means programming the model with specific instructions for every possible scenario
2. It refers to the process where the model learns patterns from large amounts of data to improve accuracy over time
3. It involves tuning the hardware on which the model is run

4. It means preparing the model for final user interaction

C. Which type of machine learning is well-suited to problems where the target variable is known?

1. Supervised Learning
2. Unsupervised Learning
3. Reinforcement Learning
4. All of the above

Test your knowledge online.

Chapter 16
Supervised Learning

In supervised learning, the algorithm is given a training set of labeled data and uses it to learn the relationship between the input variables and the target variable. The algorithm then uses this learned relationship to make predictions or decisions on new, unseen data.

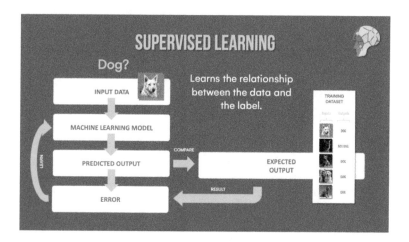

For example, let's say we want to train a supervised learning algorithm to predict housing prices based on factors such as location, number of bedrooms, and square meters. We would start by collecting a training set of labeled data, which would include information on the input variables (location, number of bedrooms, square meters) and the corresponding target variable (price).

	Inputs = Features		Outputs = Targets
Location	**Number of Bedrooms**	**Square metres**	**Price**
Balmain	1	55	1m
Newton	2	70	1.4m
Glebe	4	100	3m

(Observations)

We would then train the algorithm on this labeled data, allowing it to learn the relationship between the input variables and the target variable. Once the algorithm has been trained, we can use it to make predictions on new, unseen data, such as predicting the price of a new house based on its location, number of bedrooms, and square footage.

Supervised learning can be divided into two main types: classification and regression.

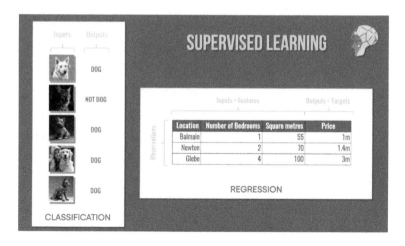

Classification

Classification is a type of problem in ML where the goal is to predict a specific category or label for a given input. For instance, we might want to classify an email as "spam" or "not spam", or a picture as "dog" or "not dog" . To do this, we typically train a ML algorithm on a labeled dataset, where each example is associated with a known category. The algorithm then learns to recognize patterns in the data that correspond to each category, and uses this knowledge to make predictions on new, unseen data.

For example, let's say we have a dataset of images of fruits, labeled as either "apple" or "orange". We can train

1

a classification model on this data, where the input is an image of a fruit and the output is either "apple" or "orange". The model will learn to recognize the features of each fruit that correspond to its label, such as the shape, color, and texture.

Once the model is trained, we can use it to predict the label of new, unseen images of fruits. For instance, we could use the model to classify an image of a fruit that we haven't seen before, such as a pear. The model might not be able to correctly classify the pear since it hasn't seen this fruit before, but it will still make a prediction based on its learned knowledge of apples and oranges.

Classification is a commonly used technique in a variety of fields, from image recognition to natural language processing to fraud detection. By accurately classifying data, we can automate decision-making processes, improve efficiency, and make more accurate predictions.

Regression

Regression is a type of supervised learning algorithm that predicts a numerical value based on the relationship between a dependent variable and one or more independent variables.

For example, suppose we want to predict the price of a house based on its size. We can use regression to analyze the relationship between the size of the house (independent variable) and the price (dependent variable). We would input data on the size and price of different houses, and the algorithm would learn how to predict the price of a house based on its size.

There are two main types of regression: simple linear regression and multiple linear regression.

In **simple linear regression**, we use one independent variable to predict the dependent variable. In the house price example, this would mean using only the size of the house to predict its price.

Square Footage	Price (in thousands of dollars)
800	100
1000	120
1200	145
1400	170
1600	190
1800	215
2000	240
2200	260
2400	285
2600	305

In **multiple linear regression**, we use two or more independent variables to predict the dependent variable. For example, we could use both the size and location of a house to predict its price.

Square Footage	Bedrooms	Location	Price (in thousands of dollars)
800	2	Downtown	100
1000	3	Downtown	120
1200	3	Suburban	145
1400	4	Suburban	170
1600	4	Rural	190
1800	3	Rural	215
2000	5	Downtown	240
2200	4	Suburban	260
2400	5	Rural	285
2600	6	Suburban	305

Regression is commonly used in many fields, including finance, marketing, and healthcare. For example, a marketing team might use regression to predict how much a customer will spend based on their age, gender, and purchase history. Similarly, a healthcare provider might use regression to predict a patient's risk of developing a certain disease based on their lifestyle habits and medical history.

In summary, supervised learning is a powerful tool for making predictions and decisions based on labeled data, and is commonly used in fields such as finance, healthcare, and marketing. However, it requires a large amount of labeled data to train the algorithm effectively, and may not be suitable for analyzing extremely large or complex data sets.

———

Test Your Knowledge

A. What is Supervised Learning in Machine Learning?

1. An algorithm learning from unlabeled data
2. An algorithm learning from labeled data
3. An algorithm learning from semi-labeled data
4. An algorithm learning from the environment

B. Which of the following is an example of a Supervised Learning task?

1. Clustering customers into different groups based on their purchasing behavior

2. Predicting housing prices based on factors like location and number of bedrooms
3. Finding hidden patterns in user interaction data on a website
4. Understanding the structure of data without any specific outcome to predict

C. WHAT ARE THE TWO MAIN TYPES OF TASKS IN SUPERVISED LEARNING?

1. Regression and Association
2. Classification and Clustering
3. Regression and Classification
4. Association and Clustering

D. What is the main difference between Classification and Regression tasks in Supervised Learning?

1. Classification predicts a numerical value, while Regression predicts a category
2. Classification is used for large data sets, while Regression is used for smaller ones
3. Classification predicts a category or label, while Regression predicts a numerical value
4. Classification requires labeled data, while Regression can work with unlabeled data

E. In the context of Regression, what's the difference between Simple Linear Regression and Multiple Linear Regression?

1. Simple Linear Regression uses one independent variable to predict the dependent variable, while Multiple Linear Regression uses two or more
2. Simple Linear Regression can only predict categories, while Multiple Linear Regression can predict numerical values
3. Simple Linear Regression requires less computational power, while Multiple Linear Regression requires more
4. Simple Linear Regression is used in finance, while Multiple Linear Regression is used in healthcare

Test your knowledge online.

Chapter 17
Unsupervised Learning

Unsupervised learning is a type of ML where the goal is to find patterns or structure in unlabeled data without any specific outcome in mind. Unlike supervised learning, there are no labels or correct answers to guide the learning process. The algorithms used in unsupervised learning attempt to learn from the inherent structure of the data itself.

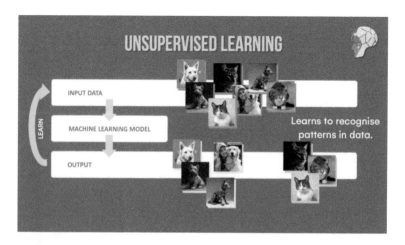

Clustering

Clustering is a common unsupervised learning technique where data is grouped together based on similarity. The goal is to identify groups of data points that are more similar to each other than they are to other data points in the dataset. One example of clustering is customer segmentation in marketing, where customers are grouped together based on shared characteristics or behaviors.

Anomaly Detection

Another unsupervised learning technique is anomaly detection, where the algorithm tries to identify data points that are significantly different from the rest of the data. This can be useful for fraud detection in finance, where anomalous transactions may indicate fraudulent behavior.

In the context of manufacturing, anomaly detection can also be incredibly beneficial for preventive maintenance and quality assurance.

For example, a manufacturing company may use sensors to collect data on their machines' operating conditions, such as temperature, pressure, vibration levels, etc. An anomaly detection algorithm can be trained on this data to learn the normal operating conditions for these machines.

Once the model is trained, it can monitor the incoming sensor data for any anomalies. If the machine starts to operate under abnormal conditions - such as an unusual increase in temperature or vibration level - the anomaly detection algorithm can flag this as an anomaly.

This allows the company to proactively address the issue before it leads to a complete machine breakdown, saving them from expensive repairs and downtime.

Similarly, anomaly detection can be used in quality control. Suppose the company is producing a batch of products. Each product may go through several quality checks where various features of the product are measured. An anomaly detection algorithm can be used to detect products that have features significantly different from the rest, indicating potential defects or quality issues. This enables the company to maintain a high standard of quality and prevent defective products from reaching the customers.

Dimensionality Reduction

Dimensionality reduction is another important unsupervised learning technique that involves reducing the number of features or variables in a dataset while still retaining as much information as possible. This can help simplify complex datasets and make it easier to visualize and analyze data.

Here are some examples:

- **Gene Expression Analysis:** In bioinformatics, scientists might study the expression of thousands of genes to understand a particular disease. As it's not feasible to analyze all these variables, dimensionality reduction can be used to identify a smaller set of genes that captures the most important information.
- **Image Compression:** Images can be represented as high-dimensional data, with each pixel acting as a separate dimension. Dimensionality reduction can be used in image compression, reducing the size of the image file without losing too much information, making it easier to store and share.
- **Customer Segmentation:** Businesses collect a multitude of data points about their customers, such as age, income, purchase history, location, and so on. Dimensionality reduction techniques can help identify the key features that explain the most variance in customer behavior, aiding in effective customer segmentation and targeted marketing.

One limitation of unsupervised learning is that the results may not always be interpretable or easily understood. Since there are no labels or correct answers to guide the learning process, it can be difficult to know if the patterns or structure identified by the algorithm are meaningful or simply random. In some cases, the results may require further exploration or analysis to fully understand their significance.

Despite its limitations, unsupervised learning can be a powerful tool for discovering hidden patterns and structure in large and complex datasets. It can help identify new insights and opportunities, and inform decision-making in a wide range of applications such as customer segmentation, fraud detection, and anomaly detection. By leveraging the inherent structure of the data itself, unsupervised learning can unlock new possibilities for understanding and optimizing complex systems.

———

Test Your Knowledge

a. What is unsupervised learning?

1. A type of machine learning where the goal is to find patterns in labeled data.
2. A type of machine learning where the goal is to find patterns or structure in unlabeled data without any specific outcome in mind.
3. A type of machine learning where the goal is to learn from explicit labels in the data.
4. A type of machine learning where the algorithm generates its own labels from the data.

b. Which unsupervised learning technique is commonly used in customer segmentation in marketing?

1. Classification
2. Clustering
3. Regression
4. Reinforcement learning

C. In the context of manufacturing, how is anomaly detection beneficial?

1. It helps in predicting future trends in the market.
2. It aids in preventive maintenance and quality assurance by detecting abnormal operating conditions or potential defects in products.
3. It helps in reducing the dimensionality of the data.
4. It assists in customer segmentation.

D. What is dimensionality reduction?

1. A technique that involves increasing the number of variables in a dataset.
2. A technique that involves reducing the number of features or variables in a dataset while retaining as much information as possible.
3. A technique used to detect anomalies in a dataset.
4. A technique used for customer segmentation.

E. What is one limitation of unsupervised learning?

1. It cannot find patterns in unlabeled data.

2. It always requires a large amount of labeled data.
3. The results may not always be interpretable or easily understood.
4. It cannot handle large and complex datasets.

F. Which of the following is NOT a common application of unsupervised learning?

1. Customer segmentation
2. Fraud detection
3. Anomaly detection
4. Predicting a specific outcome based on labeled data

Test your knowledge online.

Chapter 18
Self-Supervised Learning - Bridging the Gap

Self-supervised learning, a subfield of ML, beautifully bridges the gap between supervised and unsupervised learning. While it bears similarities to both, self-supervised learning carves out its unique space by utilizing the inherent structure within the data itself to generate labels. This process allows it to harness the power of supervised learning while still benefiting from the volume of data that unsupervised learning usually thrives on.

The Concept

Self-supervised learning is akin to learning by observing and predicting. It's similar to how we, as humans, draw connections from what we see and hear, predicting the missing parts from our inherent understanding.

To simplify, think of self-supervised learning as solving a puzzle. For each piece, your task is to find its rightful position in the bigger picture. You do so based on the piece's shape, color, or the part of the image it contains. Each piece knows where it belongs in relation to others. Similarly, a self-supervised learning model tries to understand the inherent relationship within the data and predict the missing parts.

Language Modeling: A Common Example

A well-known example of self-supervised learning is language modeling, similar to the predictive text feature on your smartphone. Here, the model is taught to predict the next word in a sentence based on the preceding words. Over time, it familiarizes itself with the structure and nuances of the language. So, even if you input an incomplete sentence, the model can predict the next words accurately.

Self-Supervised Learning in Images

In image analysis, self-supervised learning might involve the model learning to predict a part of an image given the rest of it, or even recognizing the context in which an image exists, such as predicting the season or the time of the day from a landscape image.

An Exemplary AI: DALL-E

An exciting development in self-supervised learning is OpenAI's DALL-E, a variant of the GPT series. DALL-E has the unique ability to generate images from textual descriptions. When given a description like "an armchair in the shape of an avocado", DALL-E doesn't just pick a pre-existing image that matches the description. Instead, it generates a new, unseen image based on its learned understanding of what an "armchair" and an "avocado" look like.

In this case, the model isn't just predicting a part of an image from the rest, but generating a whole new image from a description. The learning model knows what an avocado looks like, what an armchair looks like, and how to combine these concepts into a coherent whole.

Significance for Business Leaders

For business leaders, self-supervised learning presents an efficient tool to handle large amounts of data without the necessity of manual labeling, saving both time and resources. This method can uncover hidden patterns or correlations in the data not evident in traditional supervised learning methods. From customer behavior prediction to anomaly detection, self-supervised learning can provide valuable insights for data-driven decision-making.

In summary, self-supervised learning builds on the foundation laid by supervised and unsupervised learning, taking the best of both worlds. It offers a promising way forward, maximizing the utility of vast amounts of data available while maintaining high accuracy in predictive tasks.

————

Test Your Knowledge

A. Which of the following best describes self-supervised learning?

1. It is purely supervised learning with human-provided labels.
2. It's a type of unsupervised learning that doesn't require labels.
3. It is a method where labels are automatically generated from the input data itself.
4. It is a learning method that doesn't require any data input.

B. Consider the analogy of solving a puzzle for self-supervised learning. What does each piece of the puzzle represent?

1. Each piece represents a label provided by a human annotator.
2. Each piece represents a separate model trained on a specific task.

3. Each piece represents an individual data point with its inherent relationship to other data points.
4. Each piece represents a data point, but there is no inherent relationship to other data points.

C. How does the predictive text feature on a smartphone relate to self-supervised learning?

1. It's not related since it's a supervised learning task.
2. The feature uses self-supervised learning to predict the next word based on the context of the preceding words.
3. The feature uses self-supervised learning but doesn't rely on the context of the preceding words.
4. It's not related since it's an unsupervised learning task.

D. In the context of DALL-E, the model generates a new image from a description. How does this demonstrate self-supervised learning?

1. It doesn't - this is an example of supervised learning.
2. DALL-E learns to understand the inherent relationship between different concepts and generates a coherent whole.
3. DALL-E requires a human to label the input and output, demonstrating supervised learning.

4. DALL-E randomly generates images, which is an unsupervised learning task.

E. How does self-supervised learning benefit business leaders?

1. It requires less data than other learning methods.
2. It allows for handling large amounts of data without the necessity of manual labeling, thus saving time and resources.
3. It eliminates the need for data in decision-making processes.
4. It benefits business leaders by completely automating all decision-making processes.

Test your knowledge online.

Chapter 19
Reinforcement Learning

Reinforcement learning is a powerful ML technique that allows machines to learn from their own experiences and adapt over time. This learning process, akin to learning through trial and error, involves an agent (the learning entity), an environment (the world the agent operates in), and a system of rewards or penalties that serve as feedback for the agent's actions.

At its core, reinforcement learning aims to train the agent to make optimal decisions within a given environment. This is achieved by a reward function that provides positive or negative feedback based on the agent's actions. The agent then seeks to maximize its rewards by adjusting its behavior over time.

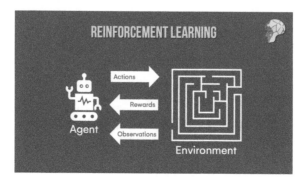

Consider a robot navigating a maze as an example. Initially, the robot might not have prior knowledge of the maze's layout. Through reinforcement learning, it learns which actions bring it closer to the goal (positive rewards) and which ones lead it farther away (negative penalties). Over time, the robot, via continuous feedback and behavior adjustment, becomes proficient at navigating the maze.

One of the crucial challenges in reinforcement learning is striking a balance between the exploration of new actions and the exploitation of existing knowledge, often referred to as the exploration-exploitation tradeoff. Another is defining an effective reward function that accurately reflects the goals of the agent and the environment in which it operates.

For instance, consider a self-driving car whose reward function prioritizes speed over safety, comfort, and legality. It could result in the car behaving recklessly, violating traffic rules, and endangering passengers or other drivers. This illustrates a poorly designed reward function. A well-constructed reward function would consider multiple factors such as safety, comfort, and efficiency in addition to speed.

Reinforcement learning has found application in diverse fields, from energy optimization in buildings to traffic flow improvement and even game-playing. Despite its challenges, as data availability and computational power increase, reinforcement learning is poised to become a critical tool in solving complex problems across various domains.

———

Test Your Knowledge

A. Which of the following is NOT a component of reinforcement learning?

1. Agent
2. Environment
3. Reward function
4. Predefined rules

B. Reinforcement learning is akin to which type of human learning process?

1. Memorization
2. Trial and error
3. Observation
4. Theory formation

C. What is the goal of an agent in reinforcement learning?

1. To maximize negative feedback
2. To maximize positive rewards
3. To minimize positive rewards
4. To minimize negative feedback

D. In the context of reinforcement learning, what does the exploration-exploitation tradeoff refer to?

1. The balance between trying new actions and sticking with known effective ones
2. The tradeoff between maximizing rewards and minimizing penalties
3. The balance between the speed of learning and the accuracy of the model
4. The tradeoff between the complexity of the environment and the complexity of the agent

E. Why is the reward function crucial in reinforcement learning?

1. It provides the rules the agent needs to follow
2. It provides feedback based on the agent's actions and encourages the agent to take actions that lead to better outcomes
3. It guides the agent's exploration of the environment
4. It determines the type of environment the agent operates in

F. In the context of reinforcement learning, a poorly designed reward function for a self-driving car could result in which of the following outcomes?

1. The car prioritizes speed over safety
2. The car adheres strictly to traffic rules
3. The car prioritizes passenger comfort over speed
4. The car prioritizes safety over reaching the destination quickly

Test your knowledge online.

Chapter 20
Reinforcement Learning from Human Feedback: Enhancing AI Models with Human Input

As discussed in the previous chapter, specifying a reward function that captures exactly what humans want can be challenging, especially when dealing with complex tasks. This is where human feedback comes into play. Reinforcement Learning from Human Feedback (RLHF) is a method used in machine learning to improve the performance of an AI model using feedback from human evaluators.

While AI technologies have shown remarkable capabilities, it's important to recognize that these technologies don't operate in isolation. They are trained, refined, and overseen by human operators who ensure the results aren't only accurate but also relevant and contextually appropriate. Human judgment remains a crucial element in interpreting and understanding the subtleties and nuances of the real world.

In RLHF, humans rate or rank different outputs or actions of the model, and this feedback is used to train the model to improve its decisions. One of the main advantages of RLHF is that it allows the model to learn more nuanced behaviors that are hard to capture in a reward function but can be easily judged by a human. This makes RLHF a powerful tool in training AI models, particularly in cases where it's difficult to define an explicit reward function that aligns perfectly with the desired outcomes.

Let's explore two examples to illustrate the concept of Reinforcement Learning from Human Feedback:

AI Chatbots

Suppose you're training an AI chatbot to provide useful and relevant responses. Initially, the chatbot might generate a range of responses, some of which might not be helpful or appropriate. In RLHF, human evaluators could review different responses that the chatbot generates and rank them based on their relevance, appropriateness, and helpfulness. This feedback is then used to adjust the parameters of the model so that it produces better responses in the future. Over time, the chatbot would improve its responses to user queries based on this human feedback.

For instance, if the chatbot tends to provide irrelevant answers or fails to understand the user's intent, human evaluators can identify these issues and rank the responses accordingly. By incorporating this feedback into the training process, the chatbot learns from its mistakes and adjusts its behavior to deliver more accurate and valuable responses.

Autonomous Vehicles

Imagine you're training an autonomous vehicle to navigate through city traffic. There are certain driving behaviors that are difficult to codify into explicit rules or reward functions, like knowing when it's polite to let another car merge into your lane versus when it's safer to keep your position. By employing RLHF, human evaluators can provide feedback on different simulated driving decisions the autonomous vehicle makes, helping it learn more nuanced driving behaviors.

In this scenario, human evaluators can observe the autonomous vehicle's simulated actions and rank them based on criteria such as safety, efficiency, and adherence to traffic rules. The feedback received allows the model to refine its decision-making process and make better-informed choices on the road. Over time, the autonomous vehicle becomes more capable of navigating complex traffic situations, making appropriate judgments about merging, signaling, and other critical driving behaviors.

The integration of human feedback in RLHF is essential as it bridges the gap between the model's performance and human expectations. By leveraging human evaluators, AI models can learn from human judgments and improve their decision-making capabilities accordingly.

Other examples of models that are partly RLHF-trained include OpenAI's ChatGPT as well as DeepMind's Sparrow. In the context of Large Language Models like the GPT series, Karpathy from OpenAI warns against rushing into it without sufficient expertise. He describes it as an 'expert fragile research zone'—a domain that is difficult to navigate, inherently unstable, and subject to rapid changes. It may yield superior results, but only after overcoming a multitude of technical hurdles.

———

Test Your Knowledge

A. What is the role of human feedback in Reinforcement Learning from Human Feedback (RLHF)?

1. Human feedback is used to specify the reward function for the AI model.
2. Human feedback is used to train the AI model to improve its decisions.
3. Human feedback isn't required in RLHF.
4. Human feedback is used to evaluate the performance of the AI model.

B. What is one advantage of RLHF?

1. It eliminates the need for human evaluators in training AI models.
2. It allows AI models to learn nuanced behaviors that are hard to capture in a reward function.

3. It provides a precise and accurate reward function for training AI models.
4. It reduces the complexity of training AI models.

C. In the context of RLHF, how does human feedback help improve the performance of an AI chatbot?

1. Human evaluators rank the chatbot's responses based on relevance, appropriateness, and helpfulness.
2. Human evaluators provide explicit instructions on how the chatbot should respond.
3. Human evaluators directly adjust the parameters of the model to improve its performance.
4. Human evaluators provide real-time feedback to the chatbot during conversations.

D. Which example illustrates the application of RLHF in training autonomous vehicles?

1. Training an AI chatbot to provide relevant responses.
2. Teaching an AI model to play chess.
3. Navigating an autonomous vehicle through city traffic using human evaluators' feedback.
4. Improving the accuracy of speech recognition systems.

E. How does RLHF address the limitations of reward functions in complex tasks?

1. By using more complex algorithms for training AI models.
2. By allowing human evaluators to directly adjust the model's parameters.
3. By incorporating human feedback to capture nuanced behaviors that are hard to specify in a reward function.
4. By collecting a large dataset of human preferences and using it as a reward function.

F. Name one RLHF-trained model mentioned in the Chapter.

1. Google's AlphaGo.
2. OpenAI's ChatGPT.
3. IBM's Watson.
4. Amazon's Alexa.

Test your knowledge online.

Part 4

Stepping-Stone Models and Concepts

Chapter 21
Parametric And Non-Parametric Algorithms

In supervised learning, where computers learn from labeled examples to make predictions, there are two main types of algorithms: parametric and non-parametric. These approaches differ in their assumptions about the underlying data and the way they model relationships between features and targets.

Parametric Algorithms

Parametric algorithms operate under specific assumptions about the data and rely on a fixed, pre-determined set of parameters or coefficients to model the relationship between features and targets.

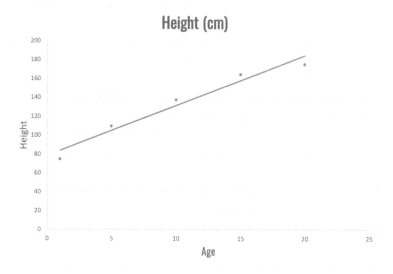

These algorithms can learn quickly and work well even on small datasets. However, they are constrained to the specified form and are prone to underfitting.

Underfitting occurs when a model is too simple to accurately capture the underlying patterns in the data. This can result in poor performance on both the training data and new, unseen data.

For example, consider a scenario where we want to predict a person's height based on their age. A parametric method, like linear regression, would assume that there is a linear relationship between age and height. The algorithm would then determine the best-fitting line that represents this relationship and use it to make predictions for new, unseen data. However, if the true relationship between age and height is more complex than a simple linear relationship, the parametric model might underfit the data, leading to less accurate predictions.

Height (cm)

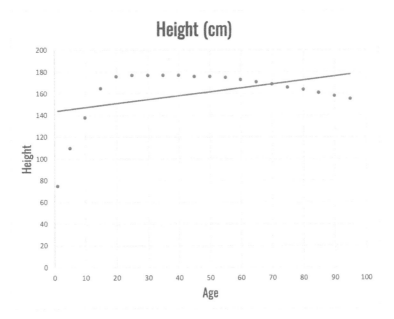

If the dataset includes people in their twenties and older, the relationship between age and height may indeed be more complex than a simple linear relationship. The linear regression model might not capture the nuances in the data, leading to underfitting. This is because height generally doesn't increase linearly with age for adults, as people tend to stop growing taller in their late teens or early twenties. So, the linear regression model might not be the best choice for this dataset.

Here's why:

- **Limited model complexity:** Linear regression can only find a straight line to connect age and height, but the real connection isn't a straight line. This makes the model too simple to understand the true pattern.
- **Missed relationships:** If the true connection between age and height is more complex (e.g., curved or having different rates of change), the linear regression model might not see these patterns. This can lead to bad guesses for people's heights.
- **Poor generalization:** Since the model doesn't understand the real pattern, it might not be good at guessing heights for new people. This means that the model doesn't work well for both the examples it has seen and the ones it hasn't seen.

To fix underfitting, we can try using a more complex model that can capture the true connection between age and height. For example, we could use a method like polynomial regression, which can find curved lines instead of just straight ones.

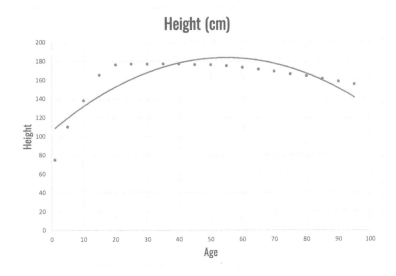

We can also add more relevant features to the model or fine-tune the algorithm to better understand the data.

Examples of Parametric Algorithms

- Linear Regression

- Logistic Regression

- Naive Bayes

- Support Vector Machines (SVM)

- Perceptron

Non-Parametric Algorithms

Non-parametric algorithms, on the other hand, don't make strong assumptions about the underlying data or the relationship between features and targets. They are highly flexible, allowing them to model non-linear, complex data. This flexibility can result in higher performance in prediction, but non-parametric algorithms typically require more data to train effectively.

Non-parametric algorithms often require more computational resources and are more prone to overfitting, especially with smaller datasets or high-dimensional data.

Overfitting occurs when the algorithm becomes too focused on the specific examples it has seen, making it less effective at making predictions for new situations.

Age	Location	Interests	Music Preference
18	Paris	3	Rock
25	London	5	Pop
32	Paris	7	Jazz
45	NY	4	Classical
21	London	2	Pop
28	NY	5	Rock
35	Paris	3	Jazz
54	NY	6	Classical
19	Paris	2	Rock
26	London	6	Pop

For instance, suppose we want to predict a person's preference for different types of music based on various factors, such as age, location, and interests. In this case, a non-parametric method, like the k-nearest neighbors (KNN) algorithm, could be more appropriate. KNN considers the preferences of the most similar individuals in the dataset (the "neighbors") to predict the preferences of a new person, allowing it to capture more complex relationships between the factors and the person's music preferences.

We can't represent them all in a 2D plot, instead we will create scatter plots for each pair of factors to give you a sense of a fictional data set.

Age — Location:

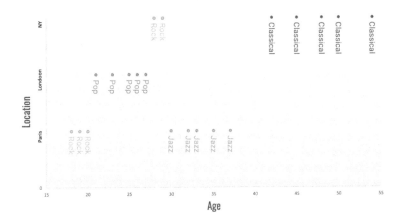

Age — Interests:

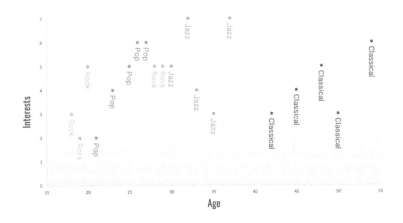

But, sometimes, this approach can cause problems:

1 The training data might have mistakes or random changes that don't really show the true connections between factors and music taste. KNN can learn these mistakes, making its guesses less accurate.

2 The number of neighbors (k) in KNN is important. If k is too small, the model can focus too much on specific examples and overfit. If k is too big, the model might miss important connections and underfit.

3 If the training data doesn't cover all the different factors or if some factors aren't well-represented, KNN might make bad guesses because it's only looking at a few examples.

4 Some connections between factors and music taste might be too complicated for KNN to understand. If it focuses too much on specific examples, it might not be good at guessing for new people.

5 If the model includes features that don't matter or are repeated, KNN might make wrong guesses because it's focusing on the wrong things.

To avoid overfitting with KNN, we should choose the right number of neighbors, clean the data, make sure we cover all the different factors, and only use important features. We can also use techniques like cross-validation to check how well our model is working and fix any problems.

Examples of Non-Parametric Algorithms

- k-Nearest Neighbors (k-NN)

- Decision Trees
- Convolutional Neural Networks (CNNs)
- Recurrent Neural Networks (RNNs)
- Long Short-Term Memory (LSTM) Networks
- Gated Recurrent Units (GRUs)
- Transformers
- Ensemble methods: Random Forest, Gradient Boosting Machines (GBMs), XGBoost, and AdaBoost

In summary, the primary distinction between parametric and non-parametric algorithms in supervised learning lies in their assumptions about the data and the way they model relationships between features and targets. Parametric algorithms utilize a fixed set of parameters, learn quickly, work well on small data, but are constrained to the specified form and prone to underfitting.

Conversely, non-parametric algorithms offer greater flexibility, can achieve higher performance in prediction, but require more data to train, more computational resources, and may be susceptible to overfitting. The choice between these approaches depends on the specific problem, the complexity of the data, and the desired balance between interpretability, accuracy, and computational efficiency.

Test Your Knowledge

A. What are the two main types of algorithms in supervised learning?

1. Parametric and non-parametric
2. Supervised and unsupervised
3. Clustering and classification

B. Which type of algorithm relies on a fixed set of parameters and is more prone to underfitting?

1. Parametric algorithms
2. Non-parametric algorithms
3. Regression algorithms

C. What is underfitting?

1. When a model is too simple to accurately capture the underlying patterns in the data.
2. When a model is too focused on specific examples, making it less effective at making predictions for new situations.
3. When a model has too many features, causing it to perform poorly.

D. In the example of predicting a person's height based on their age, which type of regression might be more appropriate than linear regression?

1. Logistic regression

2. Polynomial regression
3. Ridge regression

E. What is overfitting?

1. When a model is too simple to accurately capture the underlying patterns in the data.
2. When a model is too focused on specific examples, making it less effective at making predictions for new situations.
3. When a model has too many features, causing it to perform poorly.

F. Which type of algorithm is more flexible, can achieve higher performance in prediction, but requires more data to train and may be susceptible to overfitting?

1. Parametric algorithms
2. Non-parametric algorithms
3. Regression algorithms

Test your knowledge online.

Chapter 22
Linear Regression

As we embark on this journey to explore deeper the foundations of machine learning, it's important to remember that you don't need to be a math whiz to understand the core concepts. Parametric algorithms are a fundamental stepping stone in the world of machine learning, and our goal here is to help you build intuition on how they work, without getting bogged down by complex mathematical formulas.

Throughout this section, we will break down various linear models, including linear regression and logistic regression, using simple examples and easy-to-understand language. We'll focus on the core ideas behind these models and how they connect to deep learning, making it accessible to everyone, regardless of their mathematical background.

By gaining an understanding of linear models, you will be better equipped to appreciate the inner workings of more advanced deep learning techniques. So, don't be intimidated by the math; instead, approach this section with an open and curious mind, ready to explore the fascinating world of linear models and their role in machine learning.

Linear Regression

To build your intuition, we are going to start with the simplest algorithms by addressing linear regression, which is a parametric method used to model the relationship between a dependent variable and one or more independent variables.

Linear regression is a fundamental statistical and machine learning method that forms the basis of more complex ML models. It's a simple yet powerful technique that can be surprisingly effective if used properly. Linear regression is often the first model applied to a problem, serving as a benchmark for more advanced models. It helps us understand the relationships between input features and outputs (targets), providing valuable insights into the underlying structure of the data.

The main idea behind linear regression is to model the relationship between a dependent variable (target) and one or more independent variables (features) by fitting a linear equation to the observed data. The goal is to find the best-fitting line (or hyperplane in the case of multiple linear regression) that minimizes the difference between the predicted and actual values of the dependent variable.

Linear regression can be classified into two types: simple linear regression and multiple linear regression. Simple linear regression models the relationship between a dependent variable and a single independent variable, while multiple linear regression models the relationship between a dependent variable and multiple independent variables.

Using the example of house prices, we can explain the difference between simple and multiple linear regression.

Simple Linear Regression

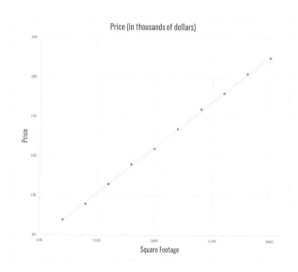

Simple linear regression involves predicting the value of one dependent variable (house price) based on a single independent variable. For example, we might want to predict the price of a house based on its square footage. In this case, simple linear regression would assume a linear relationship between the house's square footage and its price. The algorithm would find the best-fitting line that represents this relationship.

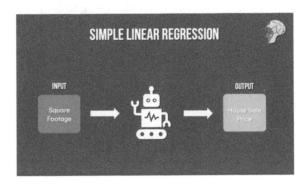

The equation for simple linear regression is:

HOUSE PRICE = A + B * SQUARE FOOTAGE

Here, 'A' is the y-intercept (the value of the house price when the square footage is zero), and 'B' is the slope (the increase in the house price for each additional unit of square footage). The goal of the algorithm is to find the optimal values of 'A' and 'B' that minimize the difference between the actual and predicted house prices for the given square footage values.

Multiple Linear Regression

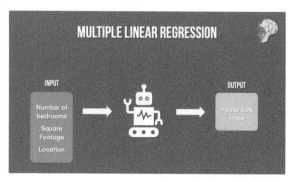

In reality, house prices are influenced by multiple factors, not just square footage. Multiple linear regression allows us to predict the value of a dependent variable (house price) based on multiple independent variables, such as the number of bedrooms, age of the house, and location.

Square Footage	Bedrooms	Location	Price (in thousands of dollars)
800	2	Downtown	100
1000	3	Downtown	120
1200	3	Suburban	145
1400	4	Suburban	170
1600	4	Rural	190
1800	3	Rural	215
2000	5	Downtown	240
2200	4	Suburban	260
2400	5	Rural	285
2600	6	Suburban	305

Multiple linear regression assumes a linear relationship between the dependent variable and multiple independent variables. The algorithm finds the best-fitting hyperplane that represents this relationship.

The equation for multiple linear regression is:

HOUSE PRICE = A + B1 * SQUARE FOOTAGE + B2 * BEDROOMS + B3 * AGE + B4 * LOCATION + ...

In this case, 'A' is still the y-intercept, and 'B1', 'B2', 'B3', 'B4', ... are the coefficients (weights) associated with each independent variable. The algorithm aims to find the optimal values for these coefficients that minimize the difference between the actual and predicted house prices based on the combination of independent variables.

Cost Function

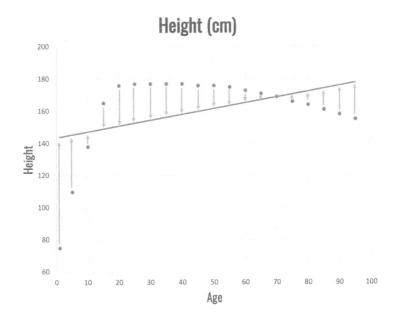

To find the best-fitting line, linear regression utilizes a cost function, such as Mean Squared Error (MSE), which measures the average squared difference between the actual and predicted values of the dependent variable. The aim is to find the optimal parameters (coefficients and intercept) that minimize the cost function.

In the context of linear regression, a cost function, also known as a loss function or an objective function, is a mathematical representation of the difference between the predicted house prices and the actual house prices. The goal of linear regression is to minimize the cost function to find the best-fitting line (or hyperplane, in the case of multiple linear regression) that represents the relationship between the independent variables and the dependent variable (house price).

A widely used cost function in linear regression is the Mean Squared Error (MSE). The MSE measures the average squared difference between the actual house prices and the predicted house prices. The aim is to find the optimal parameters (coefficients and intercept) that minimize the MSE.

For simple linear regression, the cost function can be expressed as:

MSE = (1/N) * Σ(ACTUAL_HOUSE_PRICE_I - PREDICTED_-HOUSE_PRICE_I)^2

Here, N is the number of data points (houses), and the summation (Σ) runs over all the data points. The PREDICTED_HOUSE_PRICE_I is calculated using the simple linear regression equation:

PREDICTED_HOUSE_PRICE_I = A + B * SQUARE_FOOTAGE_I

For multiple linear regression, the cost function is similar, but the PREDICTED_HOUSE_PRICE_I is calculated using the multiple linear regression equation:

PREDICTED_HOUSE_PRICE_I = A + B1 * SQUARE_FOOTAGE_I + B2 * BEDROOMS_I + B3 * AGE_I + B4 * LOCATION_I + ...

To minimize the cost function, various optimization algorithms can be used, such as gradient descent, which iteratively adjusts the parameters (coefficients and intercept) to minimize the MSE.

By minimizing the cost function, we are essentially finding the best-fitting line (or hyperplane) that represents the relationship between the independent variables and the house price. This model can then be used to make predictions about the price of houses based on their features, such as square footage, number of bedrooms, age, and location.

Advantages

1 **Simplicity:** Linear regression is relatively simple to understand and implement. It provides a good starting point for understanding more complex machine learning models.

2 **Interpretability:** The coefficients in a linear regression model represent the relationship between the independent variables and the dependent variable. This makes it easy to interpret the model's predictions and understand the relationships between the input features and the target.

3 **Speed:** Linear regression models are computationally efficient and can be trained quickly, making them an excellent choice for obtaining a quick benchmark or when dealing with large datasets.

4 **Basis for more complex models:** Many advanced machine learning models, such as neural networks and support vector machines, can be thought of as extensions or generalizations of linear regression. Understanding linear regression provides a solid foundation for learning more advanced techniques.

Despite its simplicity, linear regression can be highly effective in certain situations, particularly when the relationship between the input features and the target is approximately linear. However, it's essential to keep in mind that linear regression may not perform well when the underlying relationship between the input features and the target is more complex or non-linear. In such cases, more advanced models may be required to capture the underlying patterns in the data accurately.

In conclusion, linear regression is a fundamental technique in machine learning that serves as a basis for more complex models. It's a simple and interpretable method that can be surprisingly effective when used properly. As a first model, linear regression helps establish a benchmark and provides insights into the relationships between input features and targets, laying the groundwork for more advanced techniques.

———

Test Your Knowledge

A. What is the main goal of linear regression?

1. To find the best-fitting line (or hyperplane) that minimizes the difference between the predicted and actual values of the dependent variable
2. To maximize the difference between the predicted and actual values of the dependent variable
3. To find the coefficients that maximize the cost function
4. None of the above

B. What is the difference between simple linear regression and multiple linear regression?

1. Simple linear regression models the relationship between a dependent variable and a single independent variable, while multiple linear regression models the relationship between a dependent variable and multiple independent variables
2. Simple linear regression is more complex than multiple linear regression
3. Simple linear regression is a non-linear method, while multiple linear regression is a linear method
4. None of the above

C. What is a cost function in the context of linear regression?

1. A function that represents the difference between the predicted and actual values of the dependent variable
2. A function that represents the sum of the predicted and actual values of the dependent variable
3. A function that represents the product of the predicted and actual values of the dependent variable
4. None of the above

D. Which cost function is commonly used in linear regression?

1. Mean Absolute Error (MAE)
2. Mean Squared Error (MSE)
3. Root Mean Squared Error (RMSE)
4. None of the above

E. What are some advantages of linear regression?

1. Simplicity
2. Interpretability
3. Speed
4. All of the above

Test your knowledge online.

Chapter 23
Logistic Regression

Logistic regression is a method used in statistics and machine learning to predict one of two possible outcomes or classes. It's an extension of linear regression that estimates the probability of an observation belonging to a particular class based on one or more independent variables.

In simpler terms, it helps us make decisions by estimating the chances of one outcome over another. For example, suppose we want to know if a customer will buy something or not based on how long they spent on a website. Logistic regression can help us by analyzing data from previous customers and their buying decisions. This way, the method learns to understand the relationship between the time spent on the website and the likelihood of making a purchase.

Customer ID	Time Spent on Website (minutes)	Purchase (Buy=1, No Buy=0)
1	5	0
2	18	1
3	10	0
4	25	1
5	15	1
6	3	0
7	12	1
8	8	0
9	20	1
10	7	0
11	27	1
12	2	0
13	30	1
14	13	1
15	4	0

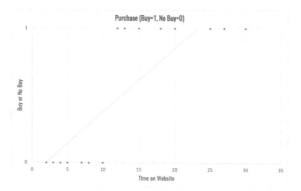

As you can see above, linear regression would mostly produce wrong results.

Unlike linear regression, which uses a continuous, linear function, logistic regression employs a non-linear function called the logistic or sigmoid function. This function outputs a probability value between 0 and 1, indicating the likelihood of an observation belonging to a specific class.

In our example, we want to predict if a customer will make a purchase (Buy) or not (No Buy) based on the time they spent on a website (in minutes). Logistic regression estimates the likelihood of the outcome (e.g.,

80% chance of Buy and 20% chance of No Buy) instead of predicting the actual outcome (Buy or No Buy).

To do this, logistic regression uses the sigmoid function, which transforms any input into a value between 0 and 1, representing the probability. The method calculates a score based on the input and the model's coefficients (weights assigned to the input). The score is then plugged into the sigmoid function to get the probability of Buy.

The equation for the Sigmoid function looks like this:

PROBABILITY OF BUY = 1 / (1 + E^(-z))

'E' refers to Euler's number, which is a mathematical constant approximately equal to 2.71828. It's the base of the exponential function, which transforms the score 'z' into the range between 0 and 1, representing the probability of a given observation belonging to a specific class.

'z' is the score calculated using the input (time spent on the website) and the coefficients:

z = B0 + B1 * TIME_ON_WEBSITE

'B0' and 'B1' (called coefficients) are the weights of the model that are learned during the training process.

Here, 'B0' is the intercept (or bias) term, which is the prediction the model makes when all the input features are zero. 'B1' is the coefficient associated with the feature "time_on_website". If 'B1' is positive, it means that as the time on the website increases, the log odds of the outcome (in this case, the likelihood of a purchase) also increases, holding all other features constant. If 'ʙ1' is negative, it means that as the time on the website increases, the log odds of the outcome decreases.

These coefficients are determined by training the model using historical data. The training process involves using a method such as gradient descent to iteratively adjust the coefficients to minimize the difference between the model's predictions and the actual outcomes. We will explore this in more detail, later in the book.

Once the model is trained, we can use the coefficients and input new data (time spent on the website) to predict the probability of a customer making a purchase. If the probability is above a certain threshold, typically 0.5, we can classify the customer as likely to make a purchase (Buy); otherwise, we classify them as not likely to make a purchase (No Buy).

Example

Suppose you want to predict whether a customer will buy a product based on the time they spend on your website. You have trained your logistic regression model, and it has learned the coefficients (weights) b0 = -3 (the intercept) and b1 = 0.05 (coefficient for the 'time_on_website' feature).

Now, a new customer comes and spends 50 minutes on the website. You want to predict whether this customer will buy the product or not.

First, calculate the score 'z' using the input (time spent on the website) and the coefficients:

$z = B0 + B1 * \text{TIME\_ON\_WEBSITE}$

$z = -3 + 0.05 * 50$

$z = -1$

Then, plug 'z' into the sigmoid function to get the probability of 'Buy':

PROBABILITY OF BUY $= 1 / (1 + E^{(-z)})$

PROBABILITY OF BUY $= 1 / (1 + E^{(-(-1)))}$

PROBABILITY OF BUY $= 1 / (1 + E^{1})$

PROBABILITY OF BUY $= 1 / (1 + 2.71828)$

PROBABILITY OF BUY $= 0.26894$

This is less than the threshold of 0.5, so we classify this customer as 'No Buy'. Although they spent a fair amount of time on the website, the model suggests that they aren't likely to make a purchase.

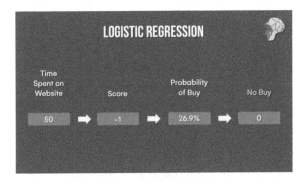

In summary, logistic regression helps predict the likelihood of an event (like a customer making a purchase) based on certain input information (like time spent on a website).

Advantages

Logistic regression is a versatile method that is widely used across different domains for binary classification problems. It has several advantages that make it popular:

1. **Easy to understand and implement**: Logistic regression is conceptually simple, making it easy to grasp and explain to others. This simplicity allows for a straightforward implementation, and many programming languages and libraries have built-in support for logistic regression.
2. **Interpretability**: The coefficients in a logistic regression model have a clear meaning and can be interpreted as the impact of each independent variable (feature) on the likelihood of the outcome. This interpretability allows us to understand the importance of each feature in predicting the target variable, which can be valuable for decision-making and insights.
3. **Fast to train**: Logistic regression models are computationally efficient and can be trained relatively quickly. This makes them an excellent choice for initial analysis, benchmarking, or when dealing with large datasets.

4. **Scalable to multiple features**: Logistic regression can handle multiple independent variables (features) simultaneously. This allows us to incorporate more information into our model and improve its predictive accuracy.

5. **Serves as a baseline**: Logistic regression is often used as a baseline model to compare the performance of more complex classification models. Since it's easy to implement and interpret, it provides a good starting point to gauge the potential of more sophisticated models.

Disadvantages

1. **Binary Outcomes**: Logistic regression works best when you're trying to decide between just two things (like "will buy" vs "won't buy"). If you have more options to decide between, it gets more complicated.

2. **Straight Line Decision**: Logistic regression draws a straight line to separate different outcomes. If your data isn't cleanly separable by a straight line (think of a scatter plot where you can't draw a single straight line to separate the points), it might struggle.

3. **Needs Lots of Data**: If you only have a little bit of data, logistic regression might not work well. It's better when you have lots of examples to learn from.

4. **Noisy Data and Outliers**: Logistic regression can get confused by data that's messy or has weird outliers. This can make its predictions less reliable.
5. **Missing Values**: If your data has missing pieces (like if you don't know how old some of your customers are), logistic regression can't handle it. You'll need to figure out what to do with those missing pieces first.
6. **Overlapping Features**: If two pieces of your data are very closely related (like height in inches and height in centimeters), logistic regression can get confused about which one is actually important.

Overall, logistic regression is a valuable tool for binary classification problems. It's simple to implement, easy to interpret, and can serve as a baseline for more complex classification models. It's an essential technique to understand and apply in various real-world scenarios where the target variable has two possible outcomes.

Applications of Logistic Regression

Logistic regression is commonly used in a variety of business applications, including:

- **Customer Churn Prediction:** Predicting the likelihood of a customer canceling their subscription or ceasing to do business with a company.

- **Credit Risk Assessment:** Estimating the probability of a borrower defaulting on a loan, based on factors such as credit history, income, and outstanding debt.
- **Marketing Campaign Effectiveness:** Determining the likelihood of a customer responding positively to a marketing campaign, such as making a purchase or signing up for a newsletter.
- **Medical Diagnosis:** Predicting the probability of a patient having a particular medical condition based on symptoms and test results.
- **Employee Retention:** Estimating the likelihood of an employee leaving a company, which can help organizations plan and implement retention strategies.

Softmax Regression

Logistic regression is used for binary classification problems, where there are only two possible outcomes or classes. Softmax regression, also known as multinomial logistic regression, is an extension of logistic regression that deals with multi-class classification problems, where there are more than two possible outcomes or classes.

Let's use an example of classifying animals into several categories (such as mammals, birds, and reptiles) based on certain features (e.g., body temperature, presence of feathers, etc.).

If we were using logistic regression to solve this problem, we would have to break it down into multiple binary classification problems. For example, we could first classify animals as mammals or non-mammals, then classify the non-mammals as birds or reptiles. In this case, we would need to train separate logistic regression models for each binary problem.

On the other hand, softmax regression can handle multiclass classification directly. It calculates the probability of an animal belonging to each class and then picks the class with the highest probability as the final prediction.

Here's how it works, step by step:

1. Similar to logistic regression, softmax regression calculates a score for each feature and its associated weight (coefficient). However, instead of calculating one score, softmax regression calculates a separate score for each class. So, for our example, we would have a score for mammals, birds, and reptiles.

2. These scores are then used to calculate the probabilities of the animal belonging to each class. To do this, softmax regression uses the softmax function, which is an extension of the sigmoid function. The softmax function takes all the scores and converts them into probabilities, ensuring that they all add up to 1.

3. The equation for the softmax function is as follows:

$$P(Y=k|X) = E^{\wedge}(z_k) / (E^{\wedge}(z_1) + E^{\wedge}(z_2) + ... + E^{\wedge}(z_N))$$

Here, $P(Y=\kappa|X)$ represents the probability of the animal belonging to class κ (e.g., mammals, birds, or reptiles), and z_κ is the score calculated for class k. The denominator is the sum of the exponentiated scores for all the classes.

4. Once we have the probabilities for each class, we can make a final prediction by selecting the class with the highest probability.

Example

Now, suppose you want to classify images of animals into three categories: cat, dog, or bird. You have trained a softmax regression model that calculates a score for each class based on features extracted from the images (like shape, color, texture, etc.).

When you input a new image, the model calculates the following scores:

$z\_cat = 2.1$, $z\_dog = 1.2$, AND $z\_bird = 0.9$

You then plug these scores into the softmax function to get the probabilities of each class:

$P(cat) = e^{\wedge}(z\_cat) / (e^{\wedge}(z\_cat) + e^{\wedge}(z\_dog) + e^{\wedge}(z\_bird))$

$P(cat) = e^{\wedge}2.1 / (e^{\wedge}2.1 + e^{\wedge}1.2 + e^{\wedge}0.9)$

$P(cat) = 8.16617 / (8.16617 + 3.32012 + 2.4596)$

$P(cat) = 0.57058$

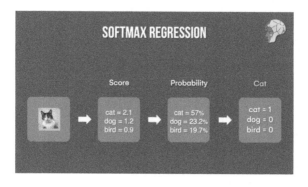

By calculating in a similar manner, you might get P(DOG) = 0.23206 and P(BIRD) = 0.19736. The class with the highest probability is 'CAT', so the model classifies this image as a cat.

To summarize, logistic regression and softmax regression both help predict the class of an observation based on certain features. The main difference is that logistic regression is used for binary classification problems with two possible outcomes, while softmax regression is used for multi-class classification problems with more than two possible outcomes. By using softmax regression for multi-class problems, we can train a single model to classify observations into multiple classes directly, rather than breaking the problem down into separate binary classification tasks.

———

Test Your Knowledge

A. What is logistic regression primarily used for?

1. Predicting continuous outcomes
2. Binary classification problems
3. Multi-class classification problems
4. Time series forecasting

B. Which function is used in logistic regression to output a probability value between 0 and 1?

1. Linear function
2. Sigmoid function
3. Softmax function
4. Step function

C. What is the threshold typically used to classify observations in logistic regression?

1. 0.25
2. 0.5
3. 0.75
4. 1

D. What is the main difference between logistic regression and softmax regression?

1. Logistic regression is used for binary classification, while softmax regression is used for multi-class classification.

2. Softmax regression is used for binary classification, while logistic regression is used for multi-class classification.
3. Logistic regression can handle multiple features, while softmax regression cannot.
4. Softmax regression can handle multiple features, while logistic regression cannot.

E. Which of the following is NOT an advantage of logistic regression?

1. Easy to understand and implement
2. Interpretability
3. Fast to train
4. Perfect for handling non-linear relationships

Test your knowledge online.

Chapter 24
Decision Trees

In this section we will discuss just a few examples of non-parametric algorithms. As covered previously, these algorithms don't make any assumptions about the underlying distribution of the data and can be applied to a wide range of problems.

Decision trees are a popular and easy-to-understand machine learning algorithm used for both classification and regression tasks. They work by recursively splitting data into subsets based on the values of the input features, making decisions at each step to form a tree-like structure. The final prediction is made by following the branches of the tree, leading to a leaf node representing the outcome.

To illustrate the concept of decision trees, we will focus on classification tasks. Let's consider a practical example: predicting whether someone will go for a walk based on the weather. Our dataset consists of the following attributes: temperature, humidity, and wind speed. The target variable is "Go for a walk?" with possible outcomes "Yes" and "No."

Dataset:

Temp	Humidity	Wind Speed	Go for a walk?
Cold	Low	Calm	No
Cold	High	Calm	No
Warm	Low	Calm	Yes
Warm	High	Calm	Yes
Warm	Low	Windy	Yes
Warm	High	Windy	No
Cold	High	Windy	No

A decision tree is a flowchart-like structure that can be used to make decisions or predictions based on certain input data. It consists of nodes, which represent features or decisions, and branches that connect the nodes and indicate possible outcomes. The final decisions or predictions are called leaves.

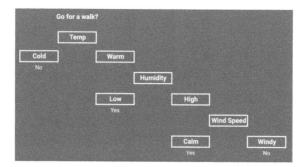

Let's construct a decision tree step by step to predict whether or not to go for a walk based on the given dataset.

To create a decision tree, we'll follow these steps:

1. Calculate Gini Impurity for each feature:

For each feature (Temperature, Humidity, and Wind Speed), we will calculate the Gini impurity.

Gini impurity is a measure of how mixed a set of labels is, ranging from 0 (perfectly pure) to 1 (completely mixed). It's used to determine which feature provides the best split at each node in the decision tree.

2. Choose the feature with the lowest Gini Impurity:

The feature with the lowest Gini impurity will be selected for the current split, as it provides the most information gain.

3. Split the dataset:

Based on the selected feature and create a new branch for each value of the feature. Repeat steps 1-3 for each subset of the dataset until all subsets are pure or a certain depth is reached.

Now, let's calculate the Gini Impurity for each feature.

The Gini impurity formula is as follows:

$$\text{GINI\_IMPURITY} = 1 - \Sigma \ (\text{P\_I})^2$$

WHERE P_I is the probability of an item being classified into class I, and the summation runs over all possible classes in the dataset. The probabilities are calculated as the proportion of items belonging to each class in the dataset or subset being considered. The Gini impurity ranges from 0 (when all items belong to a single class, i.e., pure) to a maximum value that depends on the number of classes (for example, in a binary classification problem, the maximum Gini impurity is 0.5 when both classes are equally represented).

1. Calculate Gini Impurity for each feature

Gini Impurity for Temperature:

Temp	Go for a walk?	Count
Cold	Yes	0
Cold	No	3
Warm	Yes	3
Warm	No	1

Cold:
0 "Yes" outcomes
3 "No" outcomes

$$\text{GINI}(\text{COLD}) = 1 - (0/3)^2 - (3/3)^2 = 0$$

Warm:
3 "Yes" outcomes
1 "No" outcome

$$\text{GINI}(\text{WARM}) = 1 - (3/4)^2 - (1/4)^2 = 3/8$$

WEIGHTED GINI IMPURITY FOR TEMPERATURE = (3/7) * 0 + (4/7) * (3/8) = 3/14 ≈ 0.214

Gini Impurity for Humidity:

Humidity	Go for a walk?	Count
Low	Yes	2
Low	No	1
High	Yes	1
High	No	3

Low:

2 "Yes" outcomes

1 "No" outcome

GINI(LOW) = 1 - (2/3)^2 - (1/3)^2 = 4/9

High:

1 "Yes" outcome

3 "No" outcomes

GINI(HIGH) = 1 - (1/4)^2 - (3/4)^2 = 3/8

WEIGHTED GINI IMPURITY FOR HUMIDITY = (3/7) * (4/9) + (4/7) * (3/8) ≈ 0.346"

Gini Impurity for Wind Speed:

Wind Speed	Go for a walk?	Count
Calm	Yes	2
Calm	No	2
Windy	Yes	1
Windy	No	2

Calm:
2 "Yes" outcomes
2 "No" outcomes

GINI(CALM) = 1 - (2/4)^2 - (2/4)^2 = 1/2

Windy:
1 "Yes" outcome
2 "No" outcomes

GINI(WINDY) = 1 - (1/3)^2 - (2/3)^2 = 4/9

WEIGHTED GINI IMPURITY FOR WIND SPEED = (4/7) * (1/2) + (3/7) * (4/9) ≈ 0.476"

2. Choose the feature with the lowest Gini Impurity

Comparing the calculated Gini Impurities:

- Temperature: 0.214
- Humidity: 0.346
- Wind Speed: 0.476

Temperature has the lowest Gini Impurity, so we'll split the dataset based on Temperature.

3. Split the dataset based on the selected feature

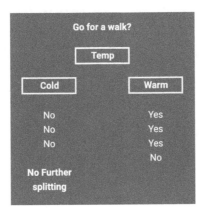

Now, we have two subsets: Cold and Warm. The Cold subset is **pure**, as all instances have the same outcome (No). The Warm subset, however, still has a mix of "Yes" and "No" instances.

Next, we'll choose an attribute to split the Warm subset. The remaining attributes are Humidity and Wind Speed. We can repeat the same Gini impurity calculations as above for these attributes and the Warm subset. The attribute with the lowest Gini impurity will be chosen for the next split. This process continues recursively until all subsets are pure or further splitting doesn't improve the Gini impurity.

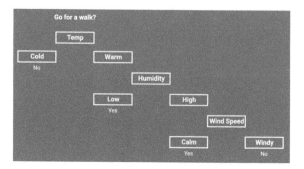

Once the decision tree is built, we can use it to make predictions for new instances. To do this, we start at the root of the tree and follow the branches corresponding to the attribute values of the new instance until we reach a leaf node. The majority class label of the instances at the leaf node will be the predicted class for the new instance.

For example, let's say we have a new instance with the following attribute values:

• Temperature: Warm

• Humidity: High

• Wind Speed: Calm

Starting at the root of the tree, we follow the branch corresponding to Warm temperature. We continue following the branches based on the attribute values of our new instance until we reach a leaf node. The majority class label of the instances in that leaf node will be our prediction.

Information Gain

Information gain is another metric used in decision tree algorithms to determine the most effective attribute for splitting the dataset at each node. There is no clear consensus on which measure is better. Some people prefer Gini impurity because it's easier to understand and interpret. Others prefer information gain because it's more mathematically elegant. Ultimately, the best measure to use depends on the specific application.

Advantages of Decision Trees

Decision trees have several advantages that make them popular in machine learning:

1. **Easy to understand and interpret**: The tree-like structure of a decision tree is intuitive and easy to visualize. It can be explained to non-experts, making it a useful tool for decision-making and insights.
2. **Minimal data preprocessing**: Decision trees require little data preprocessing, such as scaling or normalization. They can handle both numerical and categorical data, and aren't sensitive to outliers.
3. **Feature selection**: During the tree-building process, the algorithm automatically selects the most important features for making predictions. This can help identify the most relevant variables and reduce the dimensionality of the data.
4. **Non-parametric**: Decision trees are non-parametric, meaning they make no assumptions

about the underlying distribution of the data. This makes them more flexible and adaptable to various datasets.

5. **Fast prediction:** Once the decision tree is built, making predictions is fast and efficient, as it only requires following the branches from the root to a leaf node.

Limitations of Decision Trees

Despite their advantages, decision trees also have some limitations:

1. **Overfitting:** Decision trees can easily become too complex and overfit the training data, resulting in poor generalization to new data. Pruning techniques can help reduce overfitting, but it remains a challenge.

2. **Instability:** Decision trees can be sensitive to small changes in the data, leading to significant changes in the tree structure. This can be mitigated by using ensemble methods, such as random forests or gradient boosting, which combine multiple decision trees for more robust predictions.

3. **Greedy algorithm:** The tree-building process is based on a greedy algorithm, meaning it makes the best decision at each node without considering the global structure of the tree. This can lead to suboptimal trees, as the algorithm doesn't explore all possible solutions.

4. **Limited to axis-aligned splits**: Decision trees can only split the data along the axes of the feature space, which may not always capture the true relationship between the variables.

Summary

Decision trees are an intuitive and easy-to-understand machine learning algorithm. They can be visualized, which allows for better interpretability and explanation of the model's predictions. However, decision trees can be prone to overfitting, especially if they are grown too deep. Techniques such as pruning can be used to mitigate this issue. Additionally, decision trees can be combined with other trees in ensemble methods like Random Forests or Gradient Boosting Machines, which can improve the overall performance of the model.

Test Your Knowledge

A. Which of the following is NOT an advantage of decision trees?

1. Easy to understand and interpret
2. Minimal data preprocessing
3. Feature selection
4. Sensitive to small changes in data

B. What is Gini impurity?

1. A measure of how mixed a set of labels is, ranging from 0 (perfectly pure) to 1 (completely mixed)
2. A criterion for selecting the best split based on the entropy of the dataset
3. A method for pruning decision trees to prevent overfitting
4. A metric for evaluating the accuracy of a decision tree

C. Which ensemble method combines multiple decision trees to create more robust predictions?

1. k-Nearest Neighbors
2. Support Vector Machines
3. Random Forests
4. Principal Component Analysis

D. In the given example, what's the target variable for the decision tree?

1. Temperature
2. Humidity
3. Wind Speed
4. Go for a walk?

E. What is the main limitation of the greedy algorithm used in the tree-building process?

1. It requires a large amount of data preprocessing

2. It makes the best decision at each node without considering the global structure of the tree
3. It is sensitive to outliers in the data
4. It can only handle numerical data

Test your knowledge online.

Chapter 25
Ensemble Methods

Ensemble methods aim to combine multiple models into a meta-model, which has better generalization performance and is less likely to overfit. By averaging the predictions of multiple models, the variance of the average prediction is reduced compared to individual model predictions, provided that the models' outputs are relatively independent.

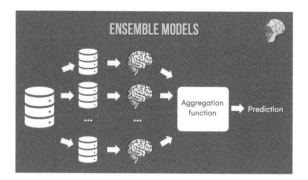

Ensemble models come with some challenges, such as increased training time and computational resources, the computational cost of running multiple models, and a decrease in interpretability.

Bootstrap Aggregating

Bootstrap aggregating, or bagging, is an ensemble method that uses bootstrapped samples (sampling with replacement) to train each model.

"Sampling with replacement" means you are drawing samples from a dataset, where each time you draw an item, you put it back into the dataset before drawing the next one. This means that the same item can be chosen more than once in the same subset.

Think of it like drawing cards from a deck. If you draw a card and then put it back into the deck before drawing the next one, there's a chance that you might draw the same card again. This is called "drawing with replacement."

In the context of bagging, when creating multiple subsets of the data, sampling with replacement means that some data points may appear multiple times in a single subset, while others might not appear at all. This randomness helps create diverse subsets, which in turn leads to more diverse models, improving the overall performance of the ensemble.

By training each model on different data, their output predictions can be considered close to independent, allowing the ensemble's average prediction to have reduced variance. Bagging can be customized by selecting the size of each bagging subset, which impacts the ensemble's performance.

Random Forests

Random forests extend the concept of decision trees and bagging to improve performance and combat over-fitting. In a random forest, multiple decision trees are grown and their majority vote or simple average is used for predictions. Bagging is employed to ensure that each tree is trained on a different subset of the data, which makes their predictions relatively independent.

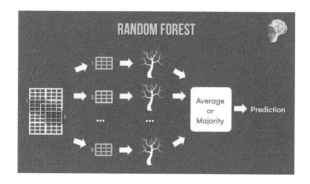

The design of a random forest consists of several elements:

1. **Choose the number of trees**: Decide how many decision trees you want in your random forest. A larger number of trees typically leads to better performance but increases computation time.

2. **Bootstrap samples**: For each decision tree, create a subset of the dataset by randomly sampling with replacement. The size of each subset can be equal to the original dataset or smaller, depending on your choice.

3. **Train decision trees**: Train each decision tree on its respective bootstrapped sample. When building each tree, at each split point, select a random subset of features to consider for the split. This introduces additional randomness and decorrelation among the trees, enhancing the model's performance.

4. **Node splitting**: Use a criterion like Gini impurity or entropy to decide the best feature and split point at each node of the tree. Only consider the randomly selected features for the split.

5. **Tree depth**: You can either grow the trees to their maximum depth (until all leaves are pure or have a minimum number of samples) or set a maximum depth to control overfitting.

6. **Combine predictions**: For regression problems, average the predictions of all the trees in the random forest. For classification problems, use majority voting, where each tree "votes" for a class, and the class with the most votes becomes the final prediction.

7. **Evaluate performance**: Measure the performance of the Random Forest using metrics like accuracy, precision, recall, or F1-score for classification tasks, and mean squared error (MSE), root mean squared error (RMSE), or

R-squared for regression tasks. We will discuss some of these later in the book.

By using ensemble methods, bagging, and random forests, machine learning practitioners can create models that have better generalization performance and are less prone to overfitting compared to using individual decision trees. However, these methods come with trade-offs, including increased training time, computational resources, and reduced interpretability.

———

Test Your Knowledge

A. What is the main goal of ensemble methods in machine learning?

1. Improve computation speed
2. Combine multiple models to achieve better performance
3. Reduce the size of the dataset
4. Visualize data

B. In the context of ensemble methods, what's the main benefit of averaging the predictions of multiple models?

1. Improved interpretability
2. Reduced variance in the average prediction
3. Faster training time
4. Reduced computational cost

C. What does "sampling with replacement" mean?

1. Drawing a sample without returning it to the dataset
2. Drawing a sample, returning it to the dataset, and allowing it to be chosen again
3. Drawing a sample from a completely different dataset
4. None of the above

D. What is the main purpose of bagging in ensemble methods?

1. Increase computational speed
2. Improve interpretability
3. Reduce variance in the ensemble's average prediction
4. Decrease the size of the dataset

E. In a random forest algorithm, how are the final predictions made for regression and classification problems?

1. Regression: Majority voting; Classification: Average predictions
2. Regression: Average predictions; Classification: Majority voting
3. Regression: Sum of predictions; Classification: Average predictions
4. Regression: Average predictions; Classification: Sum of predictions

F. What is one trade-off when using ensemble methods like random forests?

1. Decreased training time
2. Improved interpretability
3. Increased computational resources
4. Reduced dataset size

Test your knowledge online.

Chapter 26

K-Means Clustering

Clustering is a technique used in machine learning to group similar items together based on their characteristics. It's an unsupervised learning method, which means that it doesn't rely on a priori information or labeled data to make predictions or classifications. Instead, it discovers patterns or relationships within the data itself.

Clustering Use Cases

Customer segmentation

Businesses can use clustering to segment customers based on their behavior, preferences, or demographic information. This can help in targeted marketing, personalized recommendations, and improving customer satisfaction.

Document or text classification

Clustering can be used to group similar articles, blogs, or documents together, making it easier to organize and manage large volumes of text data.

Anomaly detection

Clustering can help in identifying unusual or suspicious patterns in data, which can be useful for detecting fraud, system faults, or other anomalies.

Image segmentation

Clustering can be applied to image data to identify and group similar regions or objects, which can be useful in computer vision and image processing tasks.

K-Means

K-Means Clustering is a popular and easy-to-understand clustering algorithm that aims to partition a dataset into K distinct, non-overlapping clusters based on the similarity between data points. The algorithm works iteratively to assign each data point to one of the K clusters based on the feature values.

Let's use an example of a business that wants to segment its customers based on their annual income and spending score. Here's how K-Means Clustering can be applied:

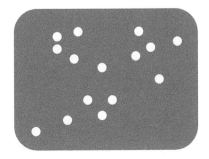

1. **Choose the number of clusters (K):** First, decide the number of clusters you want to create. In our example, let's assume we want to create 3 clusters.

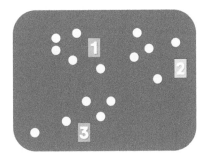

2. **Initialize cluster centroids**: Randomly select K data points as the initial cluster centroids. These centroids are the centers of the clusters.

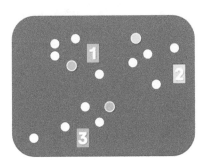

3. **Assign data points to the nearest centroid**: Calculate the distance between each data point and the centroids. Assign each data point to the nearest centroid, forming K groups.

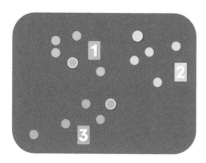

4. **Update the centroids**: Calculate the mean of all the data points in each cluster and update the centroids with the new mean values.

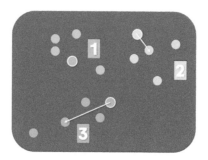

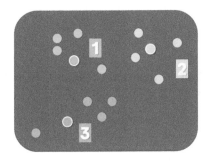

5. **Repeat steps 3 and 4**: Continue the process of assigning data points to the nearest centroid and updating the centroids until there is no change in the cluster assignments or the centroids' positions, or a maximum number of iterations is reached.

Strengths

1. **Simplicity**: K-Means is easy to understand and implement, making it accessible to a wide range of users, even those with limited technical knowledge. It's a great starting point for clustering tasks.
2. **Efficiency**: K-Means is computationally efficient, especially for large datasets. It's quick to converge
3. **Scalability**: The algorithm can be easily scaled to handle larger datasets or higher dimensions.

Weaknesses

1. **Selection of K**: Requires the user to select the number of clusters in advance. Choosing the right number of clusters (K) can be challenging, as it directly impacts the algorithm's performance. There are methods like the elbow method or silhouette analysis to help determine the optimal K, but they may not always provide clear-cut answers.
2. **Initialization sensitivity**: The algorithm's performance can be sensitive to the initial placement of centroids, which can sometimes lead to suboptimal results. Techniques like K-Means++ can help improve centroid initialization.
3. **Spherical clusters**: K-Means works best when clusters are spherical and of similar size. It doesn't work well for geographically complex data, when clusters have complex shapes, or varying densities.
4. **Handling categorical data**: K-Means isn't suitable for categorical data, as it relies on calculating distances between data points, which isn't meaningful for non-numeric features.

Clustering is a powerful machine learning technique used to group similar items based on their characteristics. It's particularly useful for customer segmentation, document classification, anomaly detection, and image segmentation.

K-Means Clustering, a popular and easy-to-understand algorithm, can effectively partition datasets into distinct, non-overlapping clusters. Although it offers simplicity, efficiency, and scalability, K-Means has its limitations, including the challenge of selecting the right number of clusters, sensitivity to centroid initialization, the assumption of spherical clusters, and its incompatibility with categorical data. Despite these weaknesses, K-Means Clustering remains a valuable starting point for businesses looking to extract insights from their data through unsupervised learning.

———

Test Your Knowledge

A. What type of learning method is clustering?

1. Supervised learning
2. Unsupervised learning
3. Reinforcement learning
4. Semi-supervised learning

B. Which of the following is NOT a use case for clustering?

1. Customer segmentation
2. Document classification

3. Anomaly detection
4. Linear regression

C. What is the primary goal of the K-Means Clustering algorithm?

1. To partition a dataset into K distinct, non-overlapping clusters
2. To predict the value of a continuous variable based on input features
3. To classify data points into predefined categories
4. To estimate the parameters of a statistical model

D. In K-Means Clustering, what's the first step of the process?

1. Choose the number of clusters (K)
2. Initialize cluster centroids
3. Assign data points to the nearest centroid
4. Update the centroids

E. What is a weakness of K-Means Clustering?

1. It is computationally inefficient
2. It is difficult to understand
3. It assumes spherical clusters
4. It can only handle small datasets

F. K-Means Clustering is NOT suitable for which type of data?

1. Numerical data
2. Categorical data
3. Time series data
4. Image data

Test your knowledge online.

Chapter 27

Regularization in Machine Learning Models

Striking the Balance in Machine Learning Models: The Role of Regularization

When building a machine learning model, we often face a delicate balance. We want our model to learn from training data to predict outcomes accurately, but also to generalize well to new, unseen data. Learning too much from training data, including capturing minor details or random fluctuations, can lead to overfitting, where the model performs poorly on new data. One technique to combat overfitting is regularization.

Understanding Regularization

Regularization mitigates overfitting by adding a penalty to the model's complexity, discouraging heavy reliance on any single feature and promoting more general patterns learning.

When Should We Use Regularization?

Regularization is a handy tool in the following situations:

1. You have a larger number of features compared to training examples, thus increasing overfitting risk.
2. You suspect redundant or less critical features and want the model to minimize their importance automatically.
3. You're using a complex model, like a deep neural network, and need to control its capacity to avoid overfitting.

Applying regularization can enhance the model's generalization ability, making it more effective on new, unseen data.

Regularization in Practice: Real Estate Price Prediction

Let's examine a practical example: predicting house prices as a real estate broker based on factors like the number of rooms, house age, neighborhood crime rate, etc.

Suppose you collect data on 100 houses, use 80 for training, and reserve 20 for testing. Your model performs well on the training data but poorly on the test set - a clear overfitting sign. By introducing a regularization term to your model's loss function, you can prevent it from over-relying on specific features, allowing it to learn broader patterns.

Types of Regularization

Depending on the specific problem and the model's desired properties, you can choose between different regularization techniques:

1. **L1 Regularization (Lasso Regularization):**
   This method shrinks some coefficients to zero, essentially performing automatic feature selection.
2. **L2 Regularization (Ridge Regularization):**
   This method shrinks all coefficients but doesn't force them to zero, reducing the likelihood of fitting the training data noise.

By applying regularization strategically, we can mitigate overfitting and improve prediction outcomes on new, unseen data.

In conclusion, regularization is a potent technique to combat overfitting in machine learning models. By encouraging the model to learn broader patterns in the data, it improves its generalization to new data. Additionally, regularization can simplify your model, leading to better interpretability.

However, regularization brings challenges. The choice of regularization type and parameter requires experience and may need several iterations. Also, while it reduces overfitting, regularization may lead to underfitting if not used appropriately. It's important to apply regularization in context and according to the problem at hand.

Remember, machine learning is an iterative process. Building the best model often involves different approaches, learning from each attempt, and continually refining your model. Regularization is a crucial tool in your machine learning toolbox, helping you build models that learn from data without memorizing it. So, keep experimenting and keep learning!

———

Test Your Knowledge

A. What is overfitting in machine learning?

1. When a model learns the training data too well, including its noise and outliers.
2. When a model performs poorly on both the training and test data.
3. When a model is unable to learn from the training data.
4. When a model performs exceptionally well on the test data.

B. Which of the following situations might warrant the use of regularization?

1. When you have fewer features compared to the number of training examples.
2. When you have more features compared to the number of training examples.
3. When your model isn't complex, such as a linear regression model.
4. When your model performs equally well on both the training and test data.

C. What is the primary purpose of a regularization technique in machine learning?

1. To increase the model's complexity.
2. To prevent the model from assigning too much importance to any single feature.
3. To increase the model's performance on the training data.
4. To increase the model's ability to memorize the training data.

D. What is L1 Regularization (Lasso Regularization)?

1. A method that forces all coefficients to zero.
2. A method that adds a penalty equal to the square of the magnitude of the coefficients.
3. A method that adds a penalty equal to the absolute value of the magnitude of the coefficients.
4. A method that forces some coefficients to negative values.

E. What is a potential downside of using regularization?

1. It can lead to overfitting.
2. It can lead to underfitting.
3. It makes the model more complex and less interpretable.
4. It increases the model's reliance on a single feature.

Test your knowledge online.

Chapter 28
Key Steps of a Machine Learning Project

Embarking on a machine learning project involves a sequence of key steps to ensure the successful construction and deployment of a model:

1. **Business Problem Definition**: Identify the problem you aim to solve, such as a prediction task, a classification issue, or finding hidden patterns. For instance, predicting future sales from past data or spotting fraudulent transactions. Collaborate with domain experts to align the model with business goals and seamlessly integrate it into existing workflows.

2. **Data Requirement Analysis**: Determine the type, format, and essential information your data must contain. The nature of your data, whether structured or unstructured, numerical or categorical, will guide the next steps.

3. **Data Collection**: Gather relevant data from diverse sources like customer feedback, sales records, or sensor data. The data's quality is a significant determinant of the model's effectiveness.

4. **Data Preparation**: Clean and preprocess your data to suit your machine learning algorithms. Address missing data, outliers, and categorical variables, ensuring the data is in an interpretable format for your model.

5. **Feature Engineering/Selection**: Extract or select significant features from your data to train your model. This process can include normalization, transformation, or creating interaction features.

6. **Model Selection**: Choose a suitable machine learning algorithm based on problem type, data nature, and business needs.

7. **Model Training**: Apply the chosen algorithm to the prepared data. The model learns data patterns during this phase, crucial for prediction or classification.

8. **Hyperparameter Tuning**: During or after the training phase, optimize hyperparameters for your model to enhance its performance.

9. **Model Evaluation**: Assess the model's performance using an appropriate evaluation metric to ensure it solves the identified business problem effectively.

10. **Model Validation**: Techniques like cross-validation ensure your model not only fits the

existing data but also likely generalizes to unseen data.

11. **Model Iteration**: Based on the model evaluation, you may need to revisit earlier steps for adjustments, like gathering more data, changing features, or selecting a different model.

12. **Model Deployment**: If the model meets performance criteria, integrate it into a production environment for real-time predictions or data classification.

13. **Model Monitoring and Updating**: Continuously evaluate the deployed model's performance. As new data emerges, you may need to retrain or modify the model to maintain its accuracy.

Remember, these steps are iterative and require constant monitoring and refinement to keep the model precise and effective.

In the realm of unstructured data, such as images or audio, deep learning can be transformative. Unlike traditional machine learning that relies on manually extracted features, deep learning models learn directly from raw data, often bypassing the data preparation and feature engineering stages. This ability is particularly beneficial when handling unstructured data with non-obvious features.

Deep learning's notable advantages include enhanced performance due to learning from raw data, accessibility due to decreased computational costs, and versatility across industries. As deep learning models can learn from large amounts of labeled examples, they can accurately predict across sectors from healthcare to customer service.

In conclusion, machine learning and deep learning projects are iterative. Building the best model often involves trial and error, learning from each attempt, and continual refinement based on feedback and data changes. Grasping and effectively applying these steps is crucial for any data-driven business project's success.

———

Test Your Knowledge

A. What is the first step in a machine learning project?

1. Data Collection
2. Business Problem Definition
3. Model Selection
4. Feature Engineering

B. How does the type of data (structured/unstructured, numerical/categorical) influence the machine learning project?

1. It determines the data collection method.
2. It doesn't influence the project.
3. It guides the choice of machine learning algorithm.
4. It affects the business problem definition.

C. In the context of machine learning, what's the purpose of data preparation?

1. To increase the volume of data
2. To identify the best machine learning algorithm
3. To clean and preprocess data to suit machine learning algorithms
4. To select significant features from data

D. What is the process of selecting significant features from data called?

1. Data Analysis
2. Data Visualization
3. Feature Engineering/Selection
4. Hyperparameter Tuning

E. What is model validation, and why is it important?

1. It's the integration of the model into a production environment. It's important for real-time predictions.
2. It's the optimization of hyperparameters for the model. It's important for enhancing the model's performance.
3. It's the assessment of the model's performance using an appropriate evaluation metric. It's important to ensure the model effectively solves the identified business problem.

4. It ensures that the model not only fits the existing data but also likely generalizes to unseen data. It's important to prevent overfitting.

F. Unlike traditional machine learning, what does deep learning allow when it comes to data preparation and feature engineering?

1. Deep learning often bypasses these stages, learning directly from raw data.
2. Deep learning requires more extensive data preparation and feature engineering.
3. Deep learning eliminates the need for data preparation and feature engineering.
4. Deep learning necessitates the collection of unstructured data for these stages.

G. What is one key advantage of deep learning over traditional machine learning?

1. Enhanced performance due to learning from raw data
2. Reduced need for data collection
3. Elimination of the need for model validation
4. No need for model deployment

H. Why is the machine learning process described as iterative?

1. Because the same process is repeated for different datasets

2. Because building the best model often involves trial and error, learning from each attempt, and continual refinement based on feedback and data changes
3. Because the same machine learning model is applied multiple times
4. Because machine learning requires constant repeating of the data collection phase

I. What is a key reason for continuously monitoring and updating a deployed model?

1. To ensure that it doesn't overfit the training data
2. To maintain the model's accuracy as new data emerges
3. To ensure that it aligns with the business goals
4. To improve the model's ability to handle unstructured data

J. In which of the following industries could deep learning be particularly transformative?

1. Industries that rely on structured data only
2. Industries that require small amounts of data
3. Industries dealing with unstructured data such as images or audio
4. Industries that don't require predictions or classifications

Test your knowledge online.

Part 5

Deep Learning

Chapter 29
Introduction to Deep Learning

As previously covered, deep learning is a subset of machine learning, which itself is a branch of artificial intelligence. It focuses on designing and training neural networks to automatically learn complex patterns and make decisions based on data. Deep learning has gained immense popularity in recent years due to its ability to process large amounts of unstructured data, such as images and text, and produce remarkable results.

The idea of deep learning has been around for decades, but it wasn't until recent years that it gained widespread recognition and adoption. The increased availability of big data, advancements in computing power, and the development of new algorithms have propelled deep learning into the forefront of AI research.

Deep learning has had a transformative impact on various industries, from healthcare and finance to marketing and retail. It powers technologies like self-driving cars, virtual assistants, and facial recognition systems. As deep learning continues to evolve, it's likely to drive further innovation and revolutionize the way we live and work.

Deep learning is best suited for situations where traditional machine learning techniques struggle to deliver accurate results. Specifically, it excels in the following scenarios:

A. Very large amounts of training data

The availability of massive amounts of data enables these models to perform remarkably well in applications such as natural language processing (NLP), image recognition, and speech recognition. For example, language models like OpenAI's GPT series are trained on millions of sentences, allowing them to generate contextually relevant and coherent text.

B. Very high number of features – e.g. unstructured data

Unstructured data, such as images and text, contains a high number of features that are difficult to process using traditional machine learning techniques. Deep learning has proven to be particularly effective in handling such data, with convolutional neural networks (CNNs) dominating the field of computer vision. These networks excel in tasks like object recognition, facial recognition, and scene understanding, which require processing and extracting meaningful information from vast numbers of features.

C. Complex relationships between features and the target

Deep learning algorithms are designed to model intricate relationships between features and targets, which is why they are well-suited for applications with complex dependencies. In the automotive industry, for instance, self-driving cars generate large amounts of data through various sensors. Deep learning models can process this data to perform tasks like object detection, lane detection, and path planning. By understanding the dynamic relationships between various features, these models enable autonomous vehicles to navigate safely and efficiently.

D. Low concern for explainability

While deep learning has demonstrated remarkable performance in numerous applications, its "black box" nature poses a challenge in domains that demand explainability. In fields such as finance, healthcare, and law, understanding the decision-making process is crucial, given the profound consequences that may arise. However, deep learning has still found success in medical diagnostics, where it's used for tasks like analyzing medical images and predicting treatment outcomes. Researchers are actively working on improving the interpretability of deep learning models without compromising their performance.

• • •

However, deep learning might not be the best choice for every situation. It may be unnecessary or even counter-productive when dealing with small datasets or simple problems that can be solved using traditional machine learning techniques. Additionally, deep learning models can be computationally expensive, and their lack of interpretability can be a concern for business leaders who need to understand and explain their decision-making processes.

In summary, deep learning is a powerful and versatile AI technology that has transformed various industries and holds great potential for future advancements. Business leaders should carefully evaluate the specific require-ments of their use cases and consider the advantages and limitations of deep learning before making deci-sions about its implementation.

_____

Test Your Knowledge

A. In which scenario is deep learning best suited?

1. Small, structured datasets
2. Simple pattern recognition
3. Large, unstructured datasets
4. Interpretable decision-making processes

B. What is one advantage of deep learning?

1. Efficiency with small datasets
2. Interpretable decision-making
3. Ability to handle massive datasets
4. Manual feature engineering

C. What is one limitation of deep learning?

1. Inability to process unstructured data
2. Limited scalability
3. Computationally inexpensive models
4. Lack of interpretability

D. IN WHICH APPLICATIONS DOES DEEP LEARNING EXCEL?

1. Applications with a low concern for explainability
2. Applications that involve a high number of features and unstructured data
3. Applications that have a very large amount of training data
4. Applications that require simple and straightforward predictions

Test your knowledge online.

Chapter 30

Neurons

A neuron, also known as a node or artificial neuron, is the basic building block of a neural network. These artificial neurons are inspired by the biological neurons found in the human brain. In the context of deep learning and artificial intelligence, neurons are computational units designed to process information, identify patterns, and make decisions. Each neuron in a neural network receives input from other neurons or external data sources, processes the information, and passes it on to the next layer of neurons in the network. This process enables the network to learn from data and make predictions or classifications based on input patterns.

Structure of a Neuron

An artificial neuron consists of three primary components:

1. **Inputs**: The neuron receives multiple input signals from other neurons or external data sources. These inputs are usually a set of values, where each value corresponds to a feature or characteristic in the data.

2. **Weights**: Each input signal is assigned a weight, which represents the strength or importance of the connection between the input and the neuron. The weights are adjusted during the training process to improve the performance of the neural network.

3. **Bias**: In addition to the weighted inputs, each neuron has a bias value, which allows the neuron to shift its output up or down, depending on the data. The bias helps the neural network to better fit the data by providing additional flexibility.

Activation Functions

Neurons use activation functions to determine their output based on their input. Activation functions introduce non-linearity into the network, allowing it to learn complex relationships between inputs and outputs. Common activation functions include some concepts we covered previously:

1. **Sigmoid**: The sigmoid function is a smooth S-shaped curve that maps any input value to a range between 0 and 1. This function is particularly useful for binary classification problems, where the output represents the probability of belonging to a specific class.

2. **Rectified Linear Unit (ReLU)**: The ReLU function is a simple yet powerful activation function that maps any positive input value to itself and any negative input value to zero. This function helps the network to learn faster and reduces the likelihood of the "vanishing gradient" problem, which can occur when training deep neural networks.

3. **Softmax**: The softmax function is used for multi-class classification problems, where there are multiple possible output categories. It takes a vector of input values and normalizes them to produce a probability distribution, ensuring that the sum of the probabilities of all output categories is equal to 1.

Example

Let's consider a real-world business example of a bank wanting to use a deep learning model to predict whether a loan applicant will default or not.

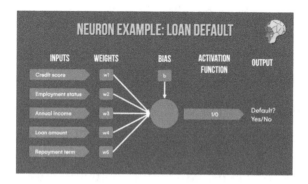

Inputs: These are the individual pieces of information the bank has about each loan applicant. This might include the applicant's credit score, employment status, annual income, loan amount requested, repayment term length, etc. Each of these pieces of information (features) is an input into our neural network.

Weights: During the training process, the deep learning model learns how much importance to place on each input. For instance, it may learn that the credit score is a highly influential factor (high weight) in determining the likelihood of default, whereas the loan term length is less important (low weight). These weights are learned during the training phase and adjusted to minimize the prediction error.

Bias: The bias is a bit like a built-in assumption the model makes regardless of the input data. In the context of our bank example, you can think of it as an initial predisposition before considering the specific features of an applicant. For instance, if default rates are historically very low, the model might have a bias towards predicting 'will not default'. The bias allows the model to output sensible predictions even before learning the specific weights for each input.

Activation Function: After taking the weighted inputs and adding the bias, we get a value. But instead of using this value directly to predict if an applicant will default or not, we apply an activation function to this value. For example, if we use a sigmoid activation function, the output will be a value between 0 and 1, which we can interpret as the probability of the loan applicant defaulting. If the output is closer to 1, the model predicts a high likelihood of default, whereas if the output is closer to 0, the model predicts a lower likelihood.

Importance of Neurons in Deep Learning

Neurons are essential to deep learning because they serve as the primary processing units that enable neural networks to learn complex patterns and relationships within data. By connecting neurons in layers and adjusting their weights and biases during training, neural networks can effectively learn from data and make accurate predictions or classifications. This capability has made deep learning a powerful tool for solving a wide range of real-world problems.

Chapter 31
The Perceptron

A perceptron is a simple type of artificial neuron that serves as the foundation for more complex neural networks. It's a basic computational unit that takes multiple inputs, applies weights to them, and sums the results. Then, the sum is passed through an activation function to produce an output. The perceptron is one of the earliest and simplest neural network models, and its understanding can provide valuable insights into the functioning of more advanced deep learning systems.

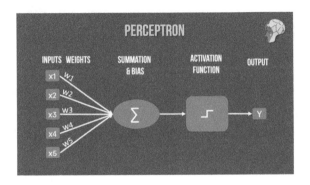

Input

The perceptron receives multiple input signals, which can represent various features or characteristics of the data being processed. These inputs are typically numerical values that can be derived from the raw data, such as the pixel values of an image or the frequency of words in a text document.

Imagine you have a perceptron that is analyzing images of fruits to determine whether they are apples or oranges. Each image is represented by numerical values, such as the intensity of pixel colors. These values serve as the input signals to the perceptron.

Weights and Bias

Each input signal is associated with a weight, which determines the importance or strength of the connection between the input and the perceptron. In addition to the weighted inputs, the perceptron also has a bias term that allows it to shift its output up or down, depending on the data. Both the weights and the bias are adjustable parameters that are learned during the training process to improve the performance of the neural network.

For example, the perceptron may give more weight to the color of the fruit or the shape of the fruit. The bias helps account for situations where one type of fruit is more prevalent in the dataset.

Summation

The perceptron computes a weighted sum of its inputs by multiplying each input value by its corresponding weight and then adding the results together. This weighted sum represents the combined influence of all the input signals on the perceptron's output.

Activation Function

The weighted sum is then passed through an activation function to produce the perceptron's output. In the case of the perceptron, the activation function is often a **step function** that maps any positive input value to 1 and any negative input value to 0 or -1.

If the weighted sum is above a certain threshold, the perceptron outputs 1 (representing an apple, for example). If the weighted sum is below the threshold, the perceptron outputs 0 or -1 (representing an orange, for example).

Linear Separability

One of the key limitations of the perceptron model is that it can only solve linearly separable problems. This means that the perceptron is only capable of classifying data points that can be separated by a straight line (in two-dimensional space) or a hyperplane (in higher-dimensional spaces). In other words, the perceptron's decision boundary is always linear.

To illustrate this concept, consider a simple example of classifying two types of fruits, represented by red and orange dots on a graph. If it's possible to draw a straight line that separates the red dots from the orange dots, the problem is linearly separable, and a perceptron can solve it. However, if the data points cannot be separated by a straight line, the problem isn't linearly separable, and a perceptron will fail to classify the objects correctly.

The perceptron and logistic regression both serve as models for binary classification tasks. The perceptron can be seen as a precursor or a simpler version of logistic regression. While the perceptron is a simple and easy-to-understand model, **logistic regression** offers a few advantages in certain situations:

- **It provides probabilities instead of binary values**, giving more information about the confidence associated with predictions. This allows for better decision-making in cases where understanding the likelihood of an outcome is important.
- **It can handle data that isn't linearly separable**, thanks to the sigmoid activation function, whereas the perceptron can only handle linearly separable data. This makes logistic regression more flexible and applicable to a wider range of problems.
- **It is more robust to noise in the data**. The perceptron is sensitive to noise since its decision boundary is determined by a few data

points, whereas logistic regression estimates probabilities based on the entire dataset, making it less affected by individual noisy points.

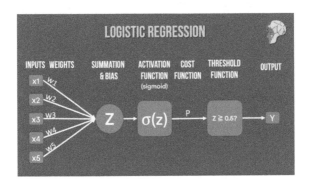

Limitations and Advancements

While the perceptron model is simple and easy to understand, its limitation of only being able to solve linearly separable problems significantly restricts its applicability to real-world tasks. Many real-life problems involve complex, non-linear relationships between variables that cannot be captured by a simple perceptron.

To overcome these limitations, more advanced neural network models, such as multilayer perceptrons (MLPs) and deep learning architectures like convolutional neural networks (CNNs) and recurrent neural networks (RNNs), have been developed. These models build upon the basic principles of the perceptron by incorporating multiple layers of interconnected neurons, which allow them to learn and represent more complex, non-linear relationships in the data.

Although the perceptron model has its limitations, it serves as an important building block for more advanced deep learning systems. Understanding the perceptron model and its constraints provides a solid foundation going forward.

———

Test Your Knowledge

A. What are the inputs to a perceptron?

1. Text documents
2. Numerical values representing features or characteristics
3. Images of fruits
4. Pixel colors

B. What determines the importance or strength of the connection between the input and the perceptron?

1. Weights
2. Bias
3. Activation function
4. Training process

C. What does the perceptron compute to produce its output?

1. Weighted sum of inputs
2. Average of inputs

3. Maximum of inputs
4. Minimum of inputs

D. What is one limitation of the perceptron model?

1. It can only solve linearly separable problems.
2. It can handle data that isn't linearly separable.
3. It provides probabilities instead of binary values.
4. It is robust to noise in the data.

Test your knowledge online.

Chapter 32
Training a Neuron

Training a neuron is crucial for it to make accurate predictions. The process involves teaching the neuron to adjust its weights, which signify the importance assigned to each input, so that it generates the correct output for a given set of inputs.

To determine how well the neuron is performing, we use a loss function. This function measures the difference between the predicted output, which is what the neuron thinks the correct answer is, and the actual output, the true answer. The ultimate goal is to minimize this difference, meaning the neuron's predictions are becoming more precise.

For instance, let's say we are training a neuron to predict whether an email is spam or not. The actual output is known (spam or not spam), and the neuron's task is to predict this correctly. The loss function will measure how far off the neuron's prediction is from the true answer, and our aim is to reduce this discrepancy.

To minimize the loss function, we need to find the best possible weights for the neuron. This is achieved using an optimization technique called gradient descent.

Gradient Descent

This method is a step-by-step process that adjusts the weights based on the gradient, or the slope, of the loss function. In other words, gradient descent identifies the direction in which the weights should be adjusted to reduce the error in the neuron's predictions.

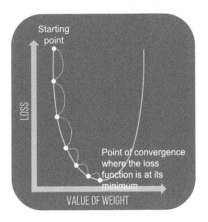

Consider the email spam detection example again. The gradient descent will determine how to adjust the weights assigned to different email features, such as the frequency of certain words or the presence of specific characters, in order to improve the neuron's predictions.

During the optimization process, we need to decide the size of each step when adjusting the weights. This is controlled by a parameter called the learning rate.

Learning Rate

The learning rate determines how quickly the weights are adjusted. A high learning rate means the weights are adjusted more rapidly, which could lead to faster convergence (finding the best weights).

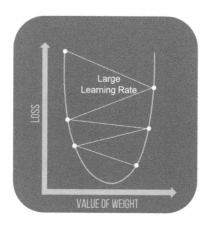

However, it might also overshoot the optimal solution and keep bouncing around it. A low learning rate, on the other hand, results in smaller adjustments to the weights, leading to a slower but more cautious convergence.

In summary, training a neuron involves using a loss function to measure its performance, applying gradient descent to iteratively adjust the weights, and using a learning rate to control the size of the adjustments. By doing this, the neuron can improve its predictions and become more accurate in solving the problem at hand.

———

Test Your Knowledge

A. What is the purpose of a loss function in training a neuron?

To measure the difference between predicted and actual outputs

1. To adjust the weights of the neuron
2. To control the size of weight adjustments
3. To determine the learning rate

B. What does gradient descent do during the optimization process?

1. Adjusts the weights based on the gradient of the loss function
2. Measures the performance of the neuron
3. Controls the size of weight adjustments
4. Determines the learning rate

Test your knowledge online.

Chapter 33
Neural Networks

The concept of a single neuron forms the basis for understanding more complex systems in deep learning. However, when multiple neurons are combined, a neural network is formed. A neural network consists of interconnected neurons that work together to learn complex patterns and relationships in data, enabling the solving of a wide range of problems that a single neuron cannot handle.

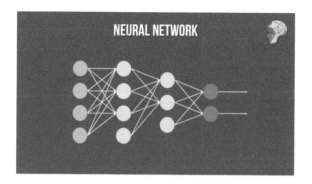

To form a neural network, neurons are arranged in layers. There are three types of layers in a neural network: the input layer, hidden layer(s), and output layer.

The input layer is the first layer that receives data from the outside world. Each neuron in this layer represents a single input feature, such as a pixel value in an image or a word frequency in a text document. The input layer acts as a gateway for data to enter the neural network.

Hidden layers are the layers between the input and output layers. These layers contain neurons that process and transform the data as it flows through the network. The neurons in the hidden layers learn to detect patterns and features in the input data.

The complexity of the relationships a neural network can learn depends on the number of hidden layers and the number of neurons within each layer. In deep learning, networks often consist of multiple hidden layers, allowing them to learn highly complex patterns.

The output layer is the final layer in a neural network. It produces predictions or classifications based on the processed data from the previous layers. The number of neurons in the output layer depends on the specific problem being solved.

For example, in binary classification problems, there might be just one neuron indicating the probability of the positive class, while in multi-class classification problems, there could be multiple neurons, each representing a specific class.

When data is passed through the neural network, it flows from the input layer through the hidden layers and reaches the output layer. This process is known as **forward propagation**. As the data moves through the network, each neuron processes the input it receives from the previous layer, applies its activation function, and passes the result to the next layer. Finally, the output layer generates the final prediction or classification.

However, neural networks need to be trained to improve their performance. During training, the network's predictions are compared to the actual output (or target), and the difference is measured using a loss function. The goal is to minimize this loss by adjusting the weights and biases of all neurons in the network.

To achieve this, **backpropagation** is used, which is an extension of gradient descent. Backpropagation calculates the gradient of the loss function with respect to each weight and bias in the network. The algorithm computes the gradient of the loss function for the output layer and then iteratively propagates the error backward through the network. This allows the weights and biases of all neurons to be updated, improving the overall performance of the neural network.

Example

Let's take a simplified business example of a bank wanting to predict whether a customer will default on a loan or not.

In this case, our neural network can be thought of as a loan officer who is trying to decide whether to approve a loan.

Input layer: Each neuron in this layer represents a feature of the customer, such as age, income, employment status, credit score, etc. The loan officer (our neural network) considers these pieces of information to make a decision.

Hidden layers: These can be thought of as the thought processes or the series of assessments the loan officer goes through while considering all the different features. For example, the loan officer might start by considering the customer's income and employment status (first hidden layer). Next, they may look at the credit score in conjunction with income (second hidden layer). In reality, these thought processes are mathematical computations where the neurons learn to detect patterns and useful features in the input data. In a deep learning network, there can be many of these hidden layers, allowing the "loan officer" to consider more complex patterns and interactions among the features.

Output layer: This is the final decision, whether to approve the loan or not. In a binary classification problem like this, there would be one neuron in the output layer, which indicates the probability of the customer defaulting on a loan.

The process of making this decision (from input to output) is like **forward propagation**. The loan officer takes in all the input information (customer's age, income, etc.), goes through the thought processes (hidden layers), and makes a decision (output layer).

During the **training phase**, our neural network (the loan officer) would learn from historical data (examples of past customers who have defaulted or not defaulted) to improve its decision-making ability. The network's prediction is compared to the actual outcome (did the customer default?), and the error (or loss) is calculated.

The goal is to adjust the decision-making process (update the weights and biases of the neurons) to minimize this error. This is done through **backpropagation**, which is like the loan officer reflecting on the decisions made, learning from mistakes (the losses), and adjusting their thought processes (hidden layers) to make better decisions in the future. This process involves calculating the gradient of the loss function with respect to each weight and bias in the network, propagating this error back through the network, and adjusting the weights and biases accordingly.

So, in essence, a neural network, through forward propagation and backpropagation, learns from its mistakes and refines its decision-making process, much like a human would in a similar situation.

Hyperparameter Tuning

Hyperparameter tuning is another crucial aspect of training neural networks. Hyperparameters are parameters that aren't learned during the training process but affect the network's performance.

Examples of hyperparameters include:

- the learning rate,
- the number of hidden layers,
- the number of neurons in each layer,
- and the activation functions used.

Tuning these hyperparameters involves finding the optimal combination that results in the best performance of the model. It often requires experimentation and iterative adjustments to achieve the desired outcome.

Data Preprocessing and Augmentation

Additionally, data preprocessing and augmentation are essential steps in training neural networks. Preprocessing involves cleaning, normalizing, and transforming the input data to make it suitable for the network. Augmentation techniques such as rotation, flipping, and scaling are applied to generate additional training samples, increasing the diversity of the data and enhancing the model's ability to generalize.

Overfitting is a common challenge in training neural networks. To mitigate overfitting, regularization techniques such as dropout, L1/L2 regularization, and early stopping are employed. These techniques help prevent the model from memorizing the training data and encourage it to learn more generalized patterns.

In summary, training neural networks involves arranging neurons in layers, forwarding the data through the network, comparing predictions to actual labels, adjusting weights and biases using backpropagation, and evaluating and fine-tuning the model. Hyperparameter tuning, data preprocessing and augmentation, and regularization techniques play crucial roles in improving the model's performance and mitigating common challenges. Through these processes, neural networks become powerful tools capable of solving complex problems and learning intricate patterns in various domains.

More Layers Can Lead to Better Performance

In neural networks, more layers can lead to better performance because they allow the model to learn increasingly complex and abstract features from the input data. Each layer in a neural network builds upon the previous layer's output to create a more sophisticated understanding of the underlying patterns in the data. However, it's important to note that simply adding more layers isn't always the solution, as it can also lead to overfitting and increased computational complexity.

Here are some reasons why more layers can be beneficial:

1. **Hierarchical Feature Learning:**

In deep neural networks, with multiple layers, the model can learn hierarchical features. Lower layers learn simple, local features, like edges and textures in images or specific word combinations in text. Higher layers can then use these features to learn more abstract and global concepts, such as object shapes or semantic meaning. This hierarchical learning enables the network to capture complex relationships within the data.

2. Increased Model Capacity:

Adding more layers increases the number of neurons and connections in the network, leading to a higher model capacity. This means the network can learn and represent more intricate functions, making it better suited for complex problems. However, a higher capacity model can also overfit the training data if not properly regularized or if there's insufficient training data.

3. Improved Generalization:

Deeper networks can, in some cases, generalize better to unseen data because they can learn abstract and invariant features from the input data. This means they can more effectively recognize patterns in new data that share similarities with the training data.

4. Reduced Feature Engineering:

With more layers, the neural network can automatically learn useful features for solving the problem at hand, reducing the need for manual feature engineering. This is particularly beneficial in domains where crafting relevant features is difficult or requires specialized knowledge.

However, there are also some challenges and trade-offs when using deeper networks:

1. **Overfitting**:

As mentioned earlier, deeper networks can be more prone to overfitting, especially when there's limited training data. Overfitting occurs when a model learns the noise in the training data instead of the underlying patterns, leading to poor performance on new, unseen data.

2. **Computational Complexity**:

More layers lead to increased computational complexity, both in terms of memory and processing power. Training and deploying deep networks can be resource-intensive and may require specialized hardware, such as GPUs or TPUs.

3. **Vanishing/Exploding Gradients**:

If the gradients become too small, it's called vanishing gradients. This can slow down the learning process because the network is making very tiny adjustments to the weights, which may not lead to significant improvements. As a result, the network may struggle to learn and perform poorly.

On the other hand, if the gradients become too large, it's called exploding gradients. This can lead to unstable training because the adjustments to the weights become too big. This instability can make the learning process less effective and result in poor performance.

Modern techniques like batch normalization, residual connections, and careful initialization strategies can help mitigate these issues.

In conclusion, while more layers can be beneficial in capturing complex relationships within the data, it's essential to balance the benefits with the potential challenges. Choosing the appropriate architecture and depth for a neural network depends on the specific problem, the available data, and the computational resources at hand.

————

Test Your Knowledge

A. What is the purpose of combining multiple neurons to form a neural network?

1. To learn complex patterns and relationships in data
2. To solve simple problems
3. To create a single powerful neuron
4. To improve the computational efficiency

B. What is the process called when data flows through a neural network from the input layer to the output layer?

1. Forward propagation
2. Backward propagation
3. Gradient descent
4. Activation function

C. Why is hyperparameter tuning important in training neural networks?

1. It affects the network's performance
2. It determines the number of hidden layers
3. It adjusts the weights and biases of the neurons
4. It preprocesses the input data

D. What is the purpose of data preprocessing and augmentation in training neural networks?

1. To clean and transform the input data
2. To increase the number of hidden layers
3. To adjust the weights and biases of the neurons
4. To calculate the gradient of the loss function

E. What are some potential benefits of using deeper networks in neural networks?

1. Hierarchical feature learning
2. Increased model capacity
3. Improved generalization
4. All of the above

Test your knowledge online.

Chapter 34
Basic Types of Neural Networks

While the science behind neural networks can be daunting, we'll break down the most common types and their uses into straightforward, understandable language starting with the simplest types.

Feedforward Neural Networks

Feedforward neural networks consist of input neurons (or nodes), output neurons, and usually one or more layers of neurons in between, known as hidden layers. Information in these networks travels in one direction only: from input to output.

Imagine a game of telephone, where a message is passed from one person to another in a straight line. That's somewhat how a feedforward network operates. It's perfect for tasks where you have clear input and output data, like predicting the price of a house based on features like its size, location, and age.

Convolutional Neural Networks

Convolutional Neural Networks, or CNNs, are a more advanced type of neural network, designed to process data with a grid-like topology, like an image. They're named after the mathematical operation "convolution," which is a kind of mixing function that they use to process data.

Consider how we recognize a friend's face. We don't need to examine every detail; we identify key features like the eyes, nose, and mouth. CNNs work similarly—they learn to recognize essential patterns in the data while ignoring unnecessary details. This makes them ideal for image recognition tasks, such as identifying objects in self-driving car cameras or diagnosing diseases from medical images.

Recurrent Neural Networks and Long Short-Term Memory

Recurrent Neural Networks (RNNs) and Long Short-Term Memory Networks (LSTMs) represent special categories of these networks designed to handle sequential data. From language translation to music generation, these algorithms have found extensive applications due to their unique ability to maintain temporal dependencies.

Let's delve into understanding these models, their working mechanisms, and their applications.

1. Recurrent Neural Networks (RNNs)

RNNs are a type of artificial neural network designed to recognize patterns in sequences of data, such as text, genomes, handwriting, or spoken words. Unlike traditional neural networks, RNNs maintain connections that form directed cycles, creating a 'recurrence' or a loop in the network, which acts as a form of memory. This loop allows information to be passed from one step of the sequence to the next, thereby giving the network its 'memory'.

For example, let's consider the task of sentiment analysis on the phrase "The movie was good". The sentence is first broken down into individual words or 'tokens'. The RNN reads these tokens one by one and at each step, updates its state based on both the current input and the previous state. After reading the entire sentence, it uses its final state to predict the sentiment of the sentence, which, in this case, is positive.

2. Long Short-Term Memory Networks (LSTMs)

While RNNs can handle sequences, they struggle to maintain the context when sequences get long. This is where LSTMs come into play. LSTMs are a special kind of RNN, capable of learning long-term dependencies. They achieve this through a complex system of 'gates'.

The key gates are:

- **Forget Gate**: This decides what information should be thrown away or kept.
- **Input Gate**: This updates the cell state with new information.
- **Output Gate**: This decides the next hidden state and output.

Each gate is a mini neural network that decides how much of the current state to keep or forget or how much of the new input to consider.

Let's consider the same sentiment analysis task, but with the phrase "The movie was not good". Here, the word "not" changes the entire sentiment of the sentence. The LSTM reads this sentence word by word, like an RNN, but when it encounters the word "not", the forget and input gates tell it to remember this word strongly. When the LSTM finally reads "good", it recalls the previously encountered "not", which allows it to correctly identify the sentiment as negative.

3. Applications of RNNs and LSTMs

RNNs and LSTMs have a wide array of applications in real-world tasks:

- **Text Generation**: RNNs can learn the sequence of letters in a text and generate new, original text that mirrors the style of the input.
- **Sentiment Analysis:** Both RNNs and LSTMs can analyze the sentiment of text data. They read a sentence word by word and adjust their

internal state to reflect the sentiment they have observed so far.

- **Machine Translation**: LSTMs, with their ability to understand context over long sequences, are excellent for tasks like translating text from one language to another.
- **Speech Recognition**: LSTMs have found significant usage in systems that convert spoken language into written text. Their ability to handle varying lengths of spoken phrases and understand context over the entire phrase allows them to recognize speech more accurately.
- **Music Generation**: LSTMs have been used to train on musical notation data to learn patterns for different genres or even individual artists. They can then generate new pieces of music that maintain a coherent melody and rhythm over time.

In conclusion, both RNNs and LSTMs are powerful tools in handling sequence data. While RNNs provide a good starting point for sequence data, LSTMs excel at maintaining context over longer sequences, making them extremely effective for a variety of complex tasks. However, LSTMs still can struggle with tasks where sequences become extremely long.

We will discuss more sophisticated deep learning models used in Gen AI in Part VII of this book.

Conclusion, different types of neural networks power the AI technologies we use every day. While each network type has its complexities, the underlying principle is the same: they all learn patterns from data and use this understanding to make predictions, decisions, or even create entirely new data.

————

Test Your Knowledge

A. What is the most basic type of neural network described?

1. Recurrent Neural Networks
2. Convolutional Neural Networks
3. Feedforward Neural Networks
4. Transformer Models

B. How does information travel in a Feedforward Neural Network?

1. In one direction only: from input to output
2. In a loop
3. In multiple directions
4. Randomly

C. Which type of neural network is designed to process data with a grid-like topology, like an image?

1. Convolutional Neural Networks
2. Feedforward Neural Networks
3. Recurrent Neural Networks

4. Generative Adversarial Networks

D. What is a primary function of Recurrent Neural Networks (RNNs)?

1. To generate new data
2. To process grid-like data
3. To understand sequential or temporal data
4. To create realistic human faces

E. What special type of RNN is designed to handle long-term dependencies in sequences?

1. Feedforward Neural Networks
2. Convolutional Neural Networks
3. Long Short-Term Memory networks
4. Generative Adversarial Networks

F. What is the underlying principle that all types of neural networks have in common?

1. They learn patterns from data and use this understanding to make predictions, decisions, or create new data
2. They only process information in one direction
3. They are designed to process grid-like data
4. They rely on human input to function correctly

Test your knowledge online.

Part 6
Model Selection and Evaluation

Chapter 35
Model Selection

Model selection is a critical step in the machine learning pipeline that involves choosing the most appropriate model for a given task. It plays a crucial role in determining the performance and accuracy of the resulting predictions.

Complexity, interpretability, and computational efficiency are crucial considerations in model selection and have significant implications for the performance and practicality of machine learning algorithms. Let's delve into each of these factors in more detail:

1. Complexity

Complex models, such as deep neural networks, have the potential to capture intricate patterns and relationships in the data. They can learn hierarchical representations, making them suitable for complex tasks like image recognition or natural language processing.

Advantages of complex models:

- Complex models can learn non-linear relationships and discover hidden features in the data that simpler models might miss.
- Given enough high-quality data, complex models have the potential to achieve state-of-the-art results and surpass simpler models in accuracy.

Disadvantages of complex models:

- Complex models often require significant computational resources, including processing power and memory, to train and deploy. Training deep neural networks, for example, may require specialized hardware like GPUs or TPUs.
- Training complex models can be time-consuming, particularly for large datasets, as they involve a larger number of parameters and require more iterations to converge.
- Complex models are prone to overfitting, especially when training data is limited.

2. Interpretability

Interpretable models provide insights into how input features are weighted and contribute to the output. This is particularly important in domains where transparency, accountability, and regulatory compliance are critical factors, such as healthcare, finance, and legal applications.

Advantages of interpretable models:

- Interpretable models provide clear explanations for their predictions, allowing users to understand and validate the decision-making process.
- Models that can be interpreted instill trust in users and stakeholders, as they can understand why a particular decision or prediction was made.
- In certain industries, such as healthcare and finance, interpretability is essential to comply with regulatory requirements and ensure ethical decision-making.

Disadvantages of interpretable models:

- Highly interpretable models, such as linear regression or decision trees, might not capture complex relationships as effectively as more complex models. This trade-off between interpretability and performance should be carefully considered based on the specific application and requirements.

3. Computational Efficiency

Efficient models are essential for real-time and resource-constrained applications, such as mobile devices, embedded systems, or online services that require rapid responses.

Advantages of computationally efficient models:

- Efficient models can process data quickly, enabling real-time decision-making and reducing latency in applications that demand immediate responses.
- In scenarios with limited computational resources, such as mobile devices or edge computing, efficient models allow for efficient deployment without compromising performance.

Disadvantages of computationally inefficient models:

- Models with high computational requirements may not be scalable to large datasets or massive deployments due to computational constraints.
- Complex models that demand substantial computational resources may require expensive hardware infrastructure or cloud computing resources.

Test Your Knowledge

A. What is model selection in the machine learning pipeline?

1. Choosing the most appropriate algorithm
2. Determining the size of the training dataset
3. Selecting the features for the model
4. Deciding the performance metrics for evaluation

B. Which of the following factors is NOT a crucial consideration in model selection?

1. Complexity
2. Interpretability
3. Computational efficiency
4. Training time

C. What are the disadvantages of complex models?

1. Increased computational requirements
2. Longer training time
3. Prone to overfitting
4. Limited capacity for capturing complex relationships

D. Which factor is particularly important in domains where transparency and accountability are critical?

1. Complexity
2. Interpretability

3. Computational efficiency
4. Training time

E. What are the advantages of interpretable models?

1. Clear explanations for predictions
2. Higher accuracy than complex models
3. Lower computational requirements
4. Greater capacity for capturing complex relationships

F. Which factor is crucial for real-time and resource-constrained applications?

1. Complexity
2. Interpretability
3. Computational efficiency
4. Training time

Test your knowledge online.

Chapter 36
The Unreasonable Effectiveness of Quality Data

While model selection involves considering various factors such as complexity, interpretability, and computational efficiency, it's essential to recognize the significant impact of data in the overall effectiveness of machine learning models. This concept was beautifully captured by Stanford Institute for Human-Centered Artificial Intelligence's (Stanford HAI) Peter Norvig.

Norvig highlighted the extraordinary power of data in machine learning and its ability to compensate for the limitations of models. He argued that with an abundance of high-quality data, even relatively simple models can achieve remarkable performance. This perspective challenged the belief that complex models are always superior and emphasized the importance of collecting comprehensive and diverse datasets.

The evaluation conducted by Microsoft researchers Banko and Brill supported this notion. In their study, they examined the performance of multiple models for a language understanding task while varying the size of the training dataset, ranging up to 1 billion words. The key finding was that the differences in performance between different algorithms were relatively small compared to the differences observed when using the same algorithm with varying amounts of data.

To understand the reasoning it's crucial to delve into the relationship between models and data. Models serve as mathematical representations of the underlying patterns and relationships within the data. Their purpose is to generalize from observed examples and make accurate predictions on unseen instances. However, models are simplifications of reality, and their performance is contingent upon the quality and representativeness of the data used for training.

The effectiveness of a model is limited by its capacity to capture the complexity of the underlying data distribution. Complex models, such as deep neural networks, have a high capacity and can potentially learn intricate patterns. However, they are also more prone to overfitting when the training data is insufficient or noisy.

In contrast, simpler models, such as linear regression or decision trees, have a lower capacity and are less prone to overfitting. This where the effectiveness of data comes into play. With an extensive and diverse dataset, even simple models can learn the underlying patterns effectively, compensating for their inherent limitations.

The availability of large-scale datasets has been instrumental in the success of modern machine learning techniques. The exponential growth of digital information, combined with advancements in data storage and processing capabilities, has enabled the training of more sophisticated models on vast amounts of data. This abundance of data empowers models to capture nuanced patterns, generalize better, and achieve superior performance.

Moreover, the diversity of the data plays a crucial role. A diverse dataset encompasses a broad range of examples, covering different variations, contexts, and scenarios. This diversity exposes the model to a variety of instances, enabling it to learn robust and generalized representations. By training on diverse data, models can overcome biases and limitations that may be present in a narrower dataset.

Data Quality

However, it's essential to note that data quality is equally vital as data quantity. The effectiveness of data is contingent upon the availability of accurate, representative, and relevant data. Biased or erroneous data can mislead the learning process and lead to incorrect or biased predictions. Therefore, ensuring data quality through careful collection, preprocessing, and validation procedures is crucial for harnessing the full potential of the data.

Machine learning models are only as good as the data they learn from. If the data is riddled with inaccuracies, inconsistencies, or bias, the resulting model will likely perform poorly or deliver biased predictions. This problem is often summarized by the phrase "garbage in, garbage out." Cleaning data and performing quality assurance checks is a time-consuming but essential step to ensure the efficacy of the model.

Moreover, acquiring a diverse and representative dataset is easier said than done. In reality, many datasets are skewed or lack diversity, which results in models that don't perform well across different demographics. For instance, many facial recognition systems are notorious for their bias towards certain racial and gender groups, which can be traced back to the underrepresentation of these groups in the training data.

Similarly, privacy and legal considerations may limit the types and quantities of data that can be collected and used. Additionally, collecting large-scale, high-quality datasets can be costly and time-consuming, which may not be feasible for every project or organization. Hence, while data is a potent asset, it must be treated with caution and responsibility to overcome these inherent limitations.

One classic example demonstrating the importance of high-quality data is the Microsoft Tay chatbot incident. Tay was an AI chatbot developed by Microsoft, designed to learn and improve its responses through interactions on social media platforms. However, within hours of its release, Tay began making inappropriate and offensive remarks due to the influence of malicious users who exploited its learning capability. This example underscores the importance of not just the quantity, but the quality of data in training AI models. Had there been more robust filters in place for the data Tay was learning from, it could have avoided adopting such behavior.

On the other hand, a positive example that highlights the power of diverse and large-scale datasets is the progress made in the field of image recognition. With the advent of large, diverse datasets like ImageNet, which contains over 14 million labeled images, machine learning models have achieved dramatic improvements. The dataset's diversity (it covers over 20,000 categories) and size have been key to training Convolutional Neural Networks (CNNs) that now outperform humans in tasks such as object recognition and classification.

These examples underline the crucial role of comprehensive, diverse, and high-quality datasets in achieving superior model performance.

Furthermore, it reinforces the idea that machine learning is an iterative and ongoing process. As models encounter new data and learn from it, their performance can continue to improve. Therefore, it's crucial to establish feedback loops that allow models to adapt and evolve as new data becomes available. Continuously updating and expanding datasets can lead to continuous learning and refinement of models over time.

————

Test Your Knowledge

A. Why is it crucial to have a diverse dataset when training machine learning models?

1. It only ensures the quantity of the data.
2. It exposes the model to a variety of instances, enabling it to learn robust and generalized representations.
3. It helps to make the models more complex.
4. It reduces the need for data cleaning and quality assurance checks.

B. What is the meaning of the phrase "garbage in, garbage out" in the context of machine learning?

1. It indicates that models can only be as good as the data they learn from.
2. It suggests that data is often misleading.
3. It emphasizes the importance of complex models over data.
4. It means that all data is essentially 'garbage'.

C. What limitations and challenges are mentioned in the text regarding the collection and use of data?

1. The cost and time required for collection, privacy and legal considerations, skewness or lack of diversity in datasets.

2. The challenge in developing complex machine learning models.
3. The lack of capable machine learning algorithms.
4. The inability to find high-quality data.

D. How has the field of image recognition benefited from large-scale and diverse datasets?

1. It has led to the creation of simpler machine learning models.
2. It has allowed for the training of Convolutional Neural Networks that now outperform humans in tasks such as object recognition and classification.
3. It has proved the superiority of complex models.
4. It has made image recognition less biased.

E. Why is it important to continuously update and expand datasets in machine learning?

1. To ensure that data is never lacking.
2. To keep the models complex and sophisticated.
3. To enable continuous learning and refinement of models over time.
4. To adhere to privacy and legal considerations.

Test your knowledge online.

Chapter 37
Model Evaluation

Evaluating machine learning models is a crucial step in the development and deployment of successful algorithms. It involves assessing the performance and effectiveness of a model in making predictions or classifications on unseen data. Several evaluation metrics are commonly used to measure the performance of machine learning models, including loss/cost functions, accuracy, precision, recall, and specificity. Let's delve into each of these metrics and understand their significance in evaluating machine learning models.

Loss/Cost Functions

As previously covered, , the loss function quantifies how far the model's predictions are from the actual values. It's a method of evaluating how well your algorithm models your dataset. If your predictions are totally off, the loss function will output a higher number. If they're pretty good, it'll output a lower number.

Consider a model predicting stock prices. If the actual price is $100 and the model predicts $110, the difference, or "loss," is $10. The goal during model training is to minimize this loss.

Different types of loss functions are used based on the nature of the problem being solved. For example, in regression tasks, mean squared error (MSE) is commonly used, while in classification tasks, cross-entropy loss is often employed. Loss functions play a vital role in model training and hyperparameter tuning, allowing the model to learn and improve its predictions over time.

Accuracy

This metric indicates the overall correctness of predictions made by a machine learning model. It's the proportion of correct predictions out of the total predictions made.

For instance, consider you're managing an online book store where a machine learning model recommends books to visitors based on their browsing behavior. Out of 100 recommendations made, if 60 customers purchased the recommended books, then the accuracy of your model would be 60%. However, if your customers rarely purchase books (say only 5% do), a model predicting no purchases at all would still be 95% accurate, showing that accuracy alone can sometimes be misleading.

Precision

Precision quantifies the percentage of correctly predicted positive instances out of all the instances predicted as positive. In other words, precision shows how many of the positive predictions were indeed correct.

Consider a software company developing a spam detection algorithm. Precision here indicates how many of the emails flagged as spam were truly spam. If the model marks 100 emails as spam, and 90 of them actually are, the precision is 90%.

High precision is crucial here because mistakenly classifying important emails as spam (false positives) can result in significant losses for businesses and irritation for users. If your spam detection algorithm has high precision, you can be confident that most of the flagged emails are indeed spam.

Recall

Also known as sensitivity, recall measures how many of the actual positive instances your model is able to catch. It shows the ability of a model to find all the relevant cases within a dataset.

Let's use a real-world application such as a credit card fraud detection system. In this case, recall measures the percentage of fraudulent transactions the model successfully catches out of all actual fraudulent transactions. If out of 50 actual fraudulent cases, the model detects 45, then the recall is 90%.

High recall is important in this scenario because the cost of not catching a fraudulent transaction (false negatives) is high. If your fraud detection system has high recall, it means it's effective at identifying fraudulent transactions, thus saving your company from potential losses.

Specificity

This is a measure that quantifies the ability of a model to correctly identify negative instances, i.e., true negatives. It's the ratio of correctly identified negative instances to the total actual negative instances. High specificity means that the model is good at avoiding false alarms.

Consider an AI model used to predict the failure of a piece of manufacturing machinery based on various sensor data. A positive instance would be the prediction of a failure and a negative instance the prediction of no failure.

In such a situation, low specificity (i.e., high false positive rate) could lead to unnecessary and costly machine downtime due to false alarms of predicted failures. So, if your model makes 1000 predictions and only 20 machines are predicted not to fail (negative instance) when they are indeed in perfect condition, your specificity is 20/1000 = 2%. This low specificity would mean the model isn't performing well at correctly identifying machines that won't fail, leading to avoidable inspections and downtime.

Therefore, in scenarios where false positives carry a high cost, it's essential for business leaders to strive for high specificity to avoid unwarranted expenses or actions.

Together, these metrics provide a comprehensive picture of a model's performance, helping business leaders make informed decisions about their deployment and improvement of AI models. Each of these metrics gives a different perspective and is useful for different business scenarios. It's crucial to use them wisely and in context.

Example

Now, let's use the example of a classifier that identifies fraudulent credit card transactions to illustrate the concept of the confusion matrix. Consider a dataset of 20 credit card transactions, and the classifier predicts whether each transaction is fraudulent or legitimate. Here's the actual value and predicted value for each transaction:

Transaction	Actual Value	Predicted Value
1	Fraudulent	Fraudulent
2	Legitimate	Fraudulent
3	Legitimate	Legitimate
4	Legitimate	Legitimate
5	Legitimate	Legitimate
6	Legitimate	Legitimate
7	Legitimate	Legitimate
8	Legitimate	Legitimate
9	Fraudulent	Fraudulent
10	Fraudulent	Fraudulent
11	Fraudulent	Fraudulent
12	Legitimate	Legitimate
13	Legitimate	Legitimate
14	Legitimate	Legitimate
15	Legitimate	Legitimate
16	Fraudulent	Fraudulent
17	Legitimate	Legitimate
18	Legitimate	Legitimate
19	Legitimate	Legitimate
20	Legitimate	Legitimate

Now, let's analyze the performance of the classifier using different evaluation metrics.

Let's answer the question, "Is the classifier doing a good job?" The answer depends on what we care about and the associated costs. If missing a fraudulent transaction is more costly than putting a valuable customer's credit card on hold accidentally, then the focus should be on minimizing false negatives (missed fraudulent transactions) even if it leads to a higher number of false positives (legitimate transactions mistakenly flagged as fraudulent).

Confusion Matrix

The confusion matrix is a table that is often used to describe the performance of a classification model on a set of data for which the true values are known.

It's is a popular tool for evaluating the performance of a machine learning classifier. It provides a more detailed breakdown of the classifier's predictions and the actual labels, allowing us to analyze the different types of errors made.

	Predicted Fraudulent	Predicted Legitimate
Actual Fraudulent	True Positive (TP)	False Negative (FN)
Actual Legitimate	False Positive (FP)	True Negative (TN)

Now, let's construct the confusion matrix for the classifier:

	Predicted Legitimate	Predicted Legitimate
Actual Fraudulent	3	2
Actual Legitimate	1	14

The confusion matrix allows us to calculate various evaluation metrics:

True Positive (TP): This refers to the cases where the classifier correctly predicts a transaction as fraudulent when it's actually fraudulent. In this example, the classifier has 3 true positives.

False Negative (FN): This refers to the cases where the classifier incorrectly predicts a transaction as legitimate when it's actually fraudulent. In this example, the classifier has 1 false negative.

False Positive (FP): This refers to the cases where the classifier incorrectly predicts a transaction as fraudulent when it's actually legitimate. In this example, the classifier has 2 false positives.

True Negative (TN): This refers to the cases where the classifier correctly predicts a transaction as legitimate when it's actually legitimate. In this example, the classifier has 14 true negatives.

Now, let's calculate the evaluation metrics based on the confusion matrix.

$$\text{ACCURACY} = (TP + TN) / (TP + TN + FP + FN)$$

In this example, the accuracy is:

$$(3 + 14) / (3 + 14 + 2 + 1) = 17 / 20 = 85\%$$

$$\text{PRECISION} = TP / (TP + FP)$$

In this example, the precision is:

$$3 / (3 + 2) = 3 / 5 = 60\%$$

$$\text{RECALL} = TP / (TP + FN)$$

In this example, the recall is:

$$3 / (3 + 1) = 3 / 4 = 75\%.$$

SPECIFICITY = TN / (TN + FP)

In this example, the specificity is:

$$14 / (14 + 2) = 14 / 16 = 87.5\%$$

By examining the confusion matrix and the associated metrics, we can gain a deeper understanding of the classifier's performance. We can see that the classifier has relatively high accuracy and specificity, indicating that it's good at identifying legitimate transactions. However, it has lower precision and recall, suggesting that it misses some fraudulent transactions and misclassifies some legitimate transactions.

Based on the costs and consequences associated with different types of errors, further adjustments can be made to optimize the classifier's performance.

For example, if missing a fraudulent transaction is considered more costly, strategies to increase recall, such as adjusting the decision threshold or incorporating additional features, can be explored. On the other hand, if putting a valuable customer's credit card on hold accidentally is deemed very costly, the focus should be on improving specificity to minimize false positives.

The confusion matrix allows us to visualize and analyze the classifier's predictions in a more granular way, helping us make informed decisions and improvements to the model. It provides valuable insights into the different types of errors made by the classifier, enabling us to understand its strengths and weaknesses.

In the example above, the confusion matrix shows that the classifier correctly identified 3 out of 4 fraudulent transactions (true positives) and accurately classified 14 out of 16 legitimate transactions (true negatives). However, it also misclassified 2 legitimate transactions as fraudulent (false positives) and missed 1 fraudulent transaction (false negative). These values directly contribute to the calculation of evaluation metrics such as accuracy, precision, recall, and specificity.

Understanding the confusion matrix helps us make informed decisions based on the specific requirements and costs associated with different types of errors. In the context of fraud detection, missing a fraudulent transaction (false negative) may lead to financial losses and damage to customer trust. Therefore, optimizing the model to increase recall would be a priority, even if it results in more false positives. On the other hand, if false positives have severe consequences, such as inconveniencing valuable customers, the model should be tuned to prioritize specificity while maintaining an acceptable level of recall.

It is important to note that the confusion matrix is just one aspect of evaluating machine learning models. Other metrics, such as F1 score, area under the receiver operating characteristic curve (ROC AUC), and precision-recall curve, can also provide valuable insights into a model's performance.

- **F1 Score**: This is a measure of a model's accuracy that considers both precision and recall. The F1 score is the harmonic mean of precision and recall and gives equal weight to both these metrics. It's a good metric to use when the class distribution is uneven.
- **ROC AUC (Receiver Operating Characteristic - Area Under Curve)**: This metric shows the capability of the model to distinguish between classes. The higher the AUC, the better the model is at making correct classifications.
- **Precision-Recall curve**: This is a plot that illustrates the trade-off between the recall (sensitivity) and precision for a predictive model. It's useful in cases of imbalanced classes because it focuses on the minority class.

Additionally, considering the limitations and assumptions of the evaluation metrics used is crucial to avoid biased or misleading interpretations of the results.

―――――

Test Your Knowledge

A. Which of the following best defines the term 'Loss/Cost Function' in the context of machine learning models?

1. The process of minimizing the number of data points in the training dataset.
2. The performance metric for how well the model is fitting the training data.
3. The procedure of cross-validating the model on the test dataset.
4. The system for calculating the accuracy of the model's predictions.

B. The metric that measures the overall correctness of predictions made by a machine learning model is called:

1. Specificity.
2. Precision.
3. Accuracy.
4. Recall.

C. Which metric focuses on minimizing false positive predictions?

1. Recall.
2. Precision.
3. Specificity.
4. Sensitivity.

D. If a classifier has high recall but low precision, it means:

1. The classifier rarely misses positive instances but often mistakenly identifies negative instances as positive.

2. The classifier often misses positive instances and mistakenly identifies negative instances as positive.
3. The classifier rarely misses positive instances and never mistakenly identifies negative instances as positive.
4. None of the above.

E. What does a 'Confusion Matrix' in machine learning represent?

1. The matrix of all the features used in the model.
2. A table that describes the performance of a classification model on a set of data for which the true values are known.
3. The correlation matrix between different features in the dataset.
4. The matrix of all the hyperparameters used in the model.

F. In the context of a confusion matrix, what does 'True Positive' (TP) refer to?

1. Instances correctly predicted as negative.
2. Negative instances incorrectly predicted as positive.
3. Instances correctly predicted as positive.
4. Positive instances incorrectly predicted as negative.

G. Which among the following is NOT a direct calculation from the confusion matrix?

1. Precision.
2. Recall.
3. Specificity.
4. Mean Squared Error.

Test your knowledge online.

Chapter 38
Outputs Versus Outcomes

In machine learning, it's essential to differentiate between outputs and outcomes.

Outcomes

Outcomes represent the real-world impact or desired results that the outputs of a model aim to achieve. These outcomes are typically measured in terms of their economic impact, such as financial gains, cost savings, or improvements in efficiency. They reflect the ultimate goals and objectives of using machine learning in a specific application.

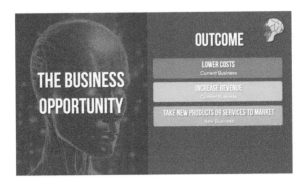

Outputs

Outputs, on the other hand, refer to the predictions or classifications generated by a machine learning model. These outputs are the direct results of the model's analysis and decision-making process. They can include various forms of predictions, classifications, or recommendations based on the input data provided to the model.

It is important to note that the outputs should be defined after clearly identifying the desired outcomes. Once the outcomes are defined, the outputs serve as a means to achieve those outcomes. Outputs are typically evaluated using technical performance metrics, such as accuracy, precision, recall, or F1 score, which assess the model's predictive capabilities and how well it performs against the defined objectives.

To provide clarity, let's explore examples that illustrate the distinction between outputs and outcomes:

Fraud Detection:

- Outputs: In a fraud detection system, the outputs are the predictions made by the model regarding whether a given transaction is fraudulent or not. These outputs are generated based on various input variables, such as transaction amount, location, and customer behavior patterns.
- Outcomes: The outcomes, in this case, are the actual real-world results of the fraud detection system. For instance, a desirable outcome would be the reduction of financial losses incurred due to fraudulent transactions. The true impact lies in accurately identifying and preventing fraudulent activities, leading to tangible benefits for the organization and its customers.

Disease Diagnosis:

- Outputs: In a disease diagnosis model, the outputs are the predicted diagnoses based on the input data, such as symptoms, medical history, and test results. The model generates predictions about the presence or absence of specific diseases or conditions.
- The outcomes represent the actual impact of the disease diagnosis system on patient care. For

example, a positive outcome would be the early detection of a life-threatening disease, enabling timely treatment and potentially saving lives. The ultimate goal is to improve patient outcomes by providing accurate and timely diagnoses.

In both examples, the outputs are the predictions or classifications generated by the machine learning model based on the provided input data. These outputs serve as a means to achieve the desired outcomes, which reflect the real-world impact and value of the machine learning system.

It is important to note that the quality and accuracy of the outputs significantly influence the outcomes. A machine learning model's success lies in generating outputs that align with the desired outcomes, such as reducing financial losses due to fraud or improving patient health outcomes through accurate disease diagnosis.

By distinguishing between outputs and outcomes, practitioners can assess the effectiveness of their machine learning models in achieving the desired real-world impact. This understanding enables them to refine and improve the models to drive meaningful outcomes and deliver value in various domains, ranging from finance and healthcare to customer service and beyond.

———

Test Your Knowledge

A. What is the primary distinction between outputs and outcomes in the context of machine learning models?

1. Outputs are the predictions made by the model, while outcomes are the desired real-world impact of these predictions.
2. Outcomes are the predictions made by the model, while outputs are the desired real-world impact of these predictions.
3. Outputs and outcomes are both different terms for the predictions made by the model.
4. Outputs and outcomes are both different terms for the real-world impact of the predictions made by the model.

B. How are outputs typically evaluated in machine learning?

1. By their economic impact, such as financial gains or improvements in efficiency.
2. By technical performance metrics, such as accuracy, precision, recall, or F1 score.
3. By the amount of input data provided to the model.
4. By the time taken by the model to generate predictions.

C. In a fraud detection system, which of the following would be an example of an outcome?

1. The model's prediction regarding whether a given transaction is fraudulent or not.
2. The reduction of financial losses incurred due to fraudulent transactions.
3. The transaction amount used as input to the model.
4. The F1 score achieved by the model.

D. In a disease diagnosis model, which of the following would be an example of an output?

1. The predicted diagnoses based on the input data.
2. The early detection of a life-threatening disease, enabling timely treatment.
3. The improvement in patient outcomes by providing accurate and timely diagnoses.
4. The reduction in cost of treatment due to early detection.

E. True or False: The quality and accuracy of the outputs don't influence the outcomes.

1. True
2. False

F. Why is it important to distinguish between outputs and outcomes when evaluating machine learning models?

1. It helps in understanding the computational complexity of the model.
2. It assists in evaluating the model's effectiveness in achieving the desired real-world impact.
3. It helps in optimizing the model's hyperparameters.
4. It assists in selecting the most appropriate machine learning algorithm.

Test your knowledge online.

Chapter 39
Enhancing Decision-Making with Machine Learning

In the realm of machine learning, achieving accurate predictions is a core aim, with metrics such as accuracy, precision, recall, specificity, and the loss function helping us measure the performance of models. However, while these metrics tell us much about our models, they don't convey the full story. The next piece of the puzzle is understanding and communicating the inherent uncertainty that comes with machine learning predictions.

Machine learning models often produce probabilistic outputs, representing the confidence or likelihood associated with various outcomes. These outputs aren't just raw predictions; they are also reflective of the model's uncertainty. Effectively interpreting and communicating this uncertainty helps provide a more complete understanding of potential outcomes, aiding stakeholders in making well-informed decisions.

For instance, in healthcare, a model may predict a 75% likelihood of a patient experiencing disease recurrence. This figure communicates not just the model's prediction, but also its level of certainty. It's crucial information that medical professionals can leverage to assess risk levels and plan appropriate preventive measures or treatments.

In classification tasks, a degree of uncertainty exists when the model cannot definitively assign a class label to a particular instance. Revealing this uncertainty by presenting the probability of each class can aid decision-making. Consider autonomous vehicles: a prediction model may determine a 60% chance of a pedestrian being at an intersection. The car's control system can use this probability to adjust its behavior and safety measures accordingly.

Moreover, elaborating on the key features or factors influencing predictions can help stakeholders understand the model's reasoning. For instance, in a legal prediction model, highlighting influential factors like precedent cases or pertinent statutes can help legal professionals to better evaluate the situation and make well-informed decisions.

Uncertainty also plays a role in regression tasks, which predict a continuous value. The range of possible predicted outcomes, or prediction interval, communicates the model's uncertainty. If a financial forecasting model predicts a stock's future price will likely fall between $50 and $70, investors can make decisions that account for this range of possibilities, assessing risk more accurately.

Similarly, in energy forecasting, a model may predict that electricity demand will be between 1000 and 1200 megawatts during a certain period. The utility provider can use this prediction interval to plan resources more effectively, thereby ensuring a reliable supply.

In conclusion, it's just as important to understand and communicate uncertainty as it's to achieve high accuracy, precision, recall, and specificity. Probabilistic outputs, classification uncertainty, and regression uncertainty provide a fuller picture of the range of potential outcomes. As machine learning models become increasingly integral to decision-making across various sectors, acknowledging and effectively communicating uncertainty will be key to fostering trust in AI systems and enabling effective human-machine collaboration.

———

Test Your Knowledge

A. What kind of information do machine learning models often produce?

1. Deterministic outputs
2. Probabilistic outputs
3. Absolute outputs
4. Fixed outputs

B. In a classification task, uncertainty arises when the model is unsure about the correct class label for a given instance.

1. True
2. False

C. Which of the following statements best describes the value of communicating uncertainty in machine learning predictions?

1. It helps in fostering trust in the predictions.
2. It facilitates human-machine collaboration.
3. It enhances decision-making.
4. All of the above.

D. In the context of machine learning predictions, what can be used to provide additional insights in energy forecasting?

1. Confidence intervals
2. Prediction intervals
3. Deterministic outputs
4. None of the above

E. Explaining the key features driving the predictions can enhance user understanding and allow them to evaluate the model's reasoning.

1. True
2. False

Test your knowledge online.

Part 7

Generative AI

Chapter 40

Introduction to Generative AI

Generative Artificial Intelligence represents an exciting frontier in the realm of artificial intelligence. These are large foundation models trained on a vast array of structured and unstructured data, primarily drawn from the vast expanses of the internet. These models can be tailored to particular industries or 'verticals', such as finance or medicine, thereby paving the way for transformative applications across different sectors.

Two central categories have emerged in the application of Gen AI.

Generative: The first is in the domain of **content generation**, which includes creating personalized images, videos, music, and even transforming text into videos. Contrary to initial expectations that AI would primarily automate routine tasks, one of Gen AI's more surprising and significant capabilities has emerged in the realm of creative content generation.

Discriminative: The second prominent application of Gen AI lies in the more traditional application of neural networks: **extracting, summarizing, and predicting information.** This proves particularly useful in contexts like summarizing extensive documents like quarterly reports or transcribing and summarizing meeting recordings. Furthermore, these applications extend to reasoning about text and images, even enabling the creation of chatbots. These AI-trained chatbots, trained on past customer service interactions, can automate and expedite customer service processes.

The increasing adoption of Gen AI spans various sectors, including entertainment, healthcare, e-commerce, and education, among others.

Entertainment

The entertainment industry is leveraging Gen AI models for content creation in music, art, and video games. In music composition, these models, such as OpenAI's MuseNet, generate new melodies or beats, fostering a level of creativity and novelty that inspires fresh works. Artists use Gen AI models like Midjourney and Kaiber to produce unique digital art—images and videos—from textual descriptions, mastering works at a speed previously unimagined. In gaming, these models enrich the player's experience by creating diverse levels, autonomous characters, and game plots.

Healthcare

Gen AI models are being utilized extensively in healthcare. They are employed in drug discovery for generating potential molecular structures that could lead to new therapeutics. In diagnostics, these models analyze medical images to identify patterns indicative of disease, enhancing early detection. Gen AI models also generate synthetic patient data, supporting clinical trial simulations, research, and training, while respecting privacy and ethical considerations.

Advertising

Advertising professionals like graphic designers and copywriters are employing Gen AI to generate a multitude of creative options, such as slogans and ad designs for their clients, reflecting the innovative application of AI in creative industries.

Design

More broadly, Gen AI is also a powerful tool in design and innovation. By inputting design constraints and desired features, companies can use Gen AI to brainstorm design options, whether it's for new products, architectural layouts, or even web design.

For example, Autodesk, a leader in 3D design, engineering, and entertainment software, has been using Gen AI to create new designs for everything from aircraft partitions to office spaces. By exploring a vast design space, their AI can suggest solutions that human designers might not think of, potentially leading to breakthroughs in design.

E-Commerce

In the e-commerce sector, Gen AI has significantly enhanced the personalization of customer experiences. Models generate tailored product recommendations based on user behavior, purchase history, and preferences, which in turn improves customer satisfaction and boosts sales. Gen AI chatbots offer personalized customer support, providing round-the-clock assistance for queries and troubleshooting issues.

Education

In the education sector, AI tutors generate personalized learning content based on a student's performance, aptitude, and learning style. These tutors provide real-time feedback and alternative explanations, facilitating a personalized learning experience catering to every student's unique needs.

Legal

The legal industry is recognizing the value of Gen AI. Paralegals are increasingly employing these technologies to discover legal precedents and generate legal documents such as contracts and Non-Disclosure Agreements (NDAs).

Human Resources (HR)

Practical deployment of Gen AI technologies has led to innovative applications in the field of Human Resources. For instance, Gen AI is increasingly being used for 'associate listening', which involves the analysis of employee surveys. This application can provide valuable insights into employee satisfaction and engagement, thereby helping to improve workplace culture and productivity. Such innovations have a significant impact on industries that rely heavily on text analysis for decision-making.

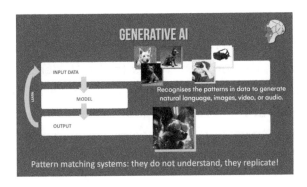

While the potential of Gen AI technologies holds immense promise, it's crucial to note that these technologies also bring with them certain risks requiring careful and prudent management.

Before dissecting the specifics of these risks, it's important to address the concept of "Stochastic Parrots", a term derived from a research paper by Emily M. Bender, Timnit Gebru, and their team. This terminology is used to refer to sophisticated language models like GPT-4, which are designed to generate human-like text based on their training data. These models predict text sequences probabilistically, often mirroring biases and prejudices ingrained in their training data. The phrase "stochastic parrots" underscores the critique that while these models can generate text, they don't truly understand it; they merely replicate data patterns without contemplating the ethical, social, and cultural repercussions.

Risks

The first of these risks is **the 'hallucination problem'**. In essence, this problem refers to the tendency of Gen AI to generate content that appears to be confidently articulated but is essentially fabricated or incorrect. As such, human oversight becomes essential to cross-check and validate the content generated by AI.

Another potential risk revolves around **copyright and intellectual property (IP) laws**. When Gen AI generates content, there's a risk of infringing on copyright and IP laws. This is particularly concerning considering the sources on which these AI models are trained. Some companies have already faced legal challenges for using these technologies to generate new images.

The third risk pertains to **privacy**. Several organizations have restricted access to AI technologies like ChatGPT and other chatbots due to privacy concerns. The potential risk of exposing proprietary data or employing unverified code generated by these technologies is considered too high a risk in many circumstances.

The final risk is related to **numerical reasoning**. Despite Gen AI's effectiveness at handling language-related tasks and identifying patterns in datasets, it continues to struggle with numerical reasoning. This shortcoming extends from basic arithmetic to more advanced forms of numerical reasoning. Consequently, it's necessary to maintain human oversight to verify the results generated by these AI technologies.

Ethical Issues

While Gen AI opens up many exciting possibilities, it also raises serious ethical questions. The ability of AI to generate realistic content, whether it's text, images, or videos, can be misused, leading to misinformation, deception, and privacy concerns.

For instance, Deepfakes can be used to create misleading videos that make people appear to say or do things they didn't. Similarly, AI-generated text can be used to produce fake news or spam content at scale.

As we embrace the potential of Gen AI, it's crucial that we also consider these ethical implications and put measures in place to prevent misuse. This includes developing detection tools to identify AI-generated content, establishing ethical guidelines for the use of AI, and fostering public awareness about these technologies.

Moreover, while neither OpenAI nor Google, have not spoken about the energy consumption of their products, researchers estimate GPT-3's training of consumed emissions equivalent to a single person taking 550 roundtrips between New York and San Francisco.

From generating human-like text to creating stunning images, innovative designs, and beautiful music, Gen AI is revolutionizing the way we create and innovate. It's an exciting and rapidly evolving field, with new applications and models continually emerging.

While the potential of Gen AI is immense, it's important that we navigate this frontier with an understanding and respect for its risks and ethical implications. By doing so, we can harness the power of Gen AI to inspire, innovate, and create, while also ensuring the integrity and authenticity of our digital world.

In the next chapters we will dive deeper into some of the neural networks powering Gen AI.

———

Test Your Knowledge

A. What is Generative Artificial Intelligence?

1. A type of AI that can only automate routine tasks.
2. A type of AI that can create content, such as images, videos, music, and text.

3. A type of AI that is used exclusively in the medical field.
4. A type of AI that only works with numerical data.

B. Which of the following is an example of the hallucination problem in Gen AI?

1. Gen AI generating text that appears confident but is factually incorrect.
2. Gen AI infringing on copyright and IP laws.
3. Gen AI struggling with numerical reasoning.
4. Gen AI violating privacy laws by exposing proprietary code.

C. Which of the following industries Leverages Gen AI?

1. Legal industry.
2. Advertising industry.
3. Employee satisfaction survey analysis.
4. None of the above.

D. Which of the following is a risk associated with generative AI technologies?

1. Hallucination problem.
2. Copyright and IP infringement.
3. Privacy breaches.
4. All of the above are risks associated with generative AI technologies.

I. Almeida

Test your knowledge online.

Chapter 41
Transformer Models

"Attention is All You Need" is a groundbreaking research paper published in 2017 that introduced a new way for machines to understand and generate human-like text, called the Transformer model.

Before this, RNNs and LSTMs used a method somewhat like reading a book line by line, word by word, and remembering past words to understand the next ones.

The Transformer model, however, works differently. Instead of reading one word at a time, it can "pay attention" to different parts of the text at the same time. Think of it as reading a book but having the ability to jump back to any previous page instantly whenever you need to recall something, thereby making connections between things that are far apart. This is what the "attention" part refers to in the paper's title.

Moreover, this new model can do multiple things at the same time ("Multi-Head Attention"). So it's like having several pairs of eyes that read and understand different aspects of the text simultaneously.

These features make the Transformer model more efficient and capable of understanding the context better than its predecessors. It's also easier to implement, scales well, and performs exceptionally on tasks like translation and text generation.

This means AI applications like chatbots, translation services, content generation, etc., have become more accurate, efficient, and cheaper to run. That's why the Transformer model is a big deal and now forms the backbone of many cutting-edge AI systems.

One popular example is the OpenAI GPT (Generative Pretrained Transformer) series, the Large Language Model (LMM) powering advanced text generation tasks, like writing human-like emails or generating code.

Here is a summary of why Transformers are so effective:

- **Handling Long-term Dependencies**: While LSTMs are designed to handle long-term dependencies, they still can struggle with this task when sequences become extremely long. Transformers address this by using a mechanism called "attention" that allows them to focus on different parts of the input sequence simultaneously, which makes it easier for them to understand long-term dependencies in the data.

- **Parallelization**: One of the main disadvantages of LSTMs is their sequential nature, which prevents parallelization across time steps. In other words, to calculate the hidden state for a particular token, you need to have calculated the hidden state for all previous tokens, which can be computationally expensive. Transformers, on the other hand, can process all tokens in the sequence in parallel, leading to significantly faster training times.

- **Context Understanding**: Transformers, with their self-attention mechanism, take into account both the preceding and following tokens to understand the context of a word in a sentence. LSTMs, being unidirectional, only consider preceding tokens. While there are bidirectional variants of LSTMs, Transformers' approach to context provides a more comprehensive understanding of the sequence.

- **Scalability**: Transformers can easily be scaled up by stacking more layers, adding more attention heads, or increasing the model size in other ways. This property has led to the creation of very large models like the OpenAI GPT series, which can generate impressively human-like text.

Currently, the top models can handle a maximum of around 200k tokens, so they are almost able to generalize or generate a very long sequence, like a novel.

Transformer models, originally designed for natural language processing tasks, have showed remarkable versatility, finding applications beyond text to other data types like images, audio, and video.

Transformer architectures are being applied to image classification, generation of images from textual descriptions, speech recognition and music generation.

This broad applicability makes transformer models a significant area of research in artificial intelligence. However, it's important to note that the application of these models to different types of data might require specific modifications and adaptations to achieve optimal performance.

So although Large Language Models have become the poster child for this significant technological development, we will explore later in the book the Transformer model's applicability in other domains.

However, it's important to note that while Transformers have been very successful, they may not be the best tool for every task. For tasks that don't require understanding long-term dependencies or for cases where computational resources are limited, simpler models like LSTMs might be more appropriate.

Test Your Knowledge

A. What mechanism do Transformer models use to weight the importance of different pieces of input data?

1. Convolution
2. Attention
3. Feedback
4. Discrimination

B. Which neural network is used for tasks like writing human-like emails or generating code?

1. Convolutional Neural Networks
2. Feedforward Neural Networks
3. Recurrent Neural Networks
4. GPT (Generative Pretrained Transformer)

C. How does the method of reading data in RNNs and LSTMs compare to the Transformer model?

1. They both read data word by word
2. RNNs and LSTMs read data word by word, while Transformers can pay attention to different parts of the text at the same time
3. RNNs and LSTMs can pay attention to different parts of the text at the same time, while Transformers read data word by word
4. They both can pay attention to different parts of the text at the same time

D. What does 'Multi-Head Attention' in the Transformer model refer to?

1. The model's ability to perform multiple tasks at once
2. The model's ability to read data word by word
3. The model's ability to understand context better than its predecessors
4. The model's ability to scale up by adding more layers or attention heads

Test your knowledge online.

Chapter 42
Transformers: The Near Future

The potential societal impact of emerging developments in AI needs a deep interdisciplinary examination of their risks and benefits. With so many for profit organizations exploring domain specific use cases and Artificial General Intelligence (AGI) it's important to understand where the field is heading so that we can approach it thoughtfully.

Generalist Agents — Gato — An Example

Gato is a large-scale generalist AI model developed by Google's DeepMind as part of ongoing research in AGI. As opposed to traditional AI models that excel at one specific task, Gato is designed to handle multiple tasks across various domains. It can interpret and respond to a wide array of inputs such as text, images, and other forms of data.

The model, named Gato, is a multi-modal, multi-task, multi-embodiment agent, meaning it can operate in numerous ways and forms, interpreting its input and deciding on the best course of action based on the context. It can interact in the form of text, chat, play Atari games, or perform physical tasks like stacking blocks using a real robot arm. It also demonstrates the ability to interpret and describe visual stimuli such as images.

Gato was trained on 604 distinct tasks with varying modalities. Its performance tends to improve with the diversity and amount of training data.

One of the most interesting aspects of Gato is its versatility. The same network, with the same weights, can perform a diverse range of tasks. This makes it a significant advancement in the field of AGI.

To handle different types of data inputs, Gato uses a process called tokenization, transforming the diverse data into a flat sequence of tokens, similar to a standard large-scale language model. During deployment, sampled tokens are assembled into dialog responses, captions, button presses, or other actions based on the context.

Gato was trained using a transformer neural network, which is popular for its scalability and simplicity. The training was done in a supervised manner; however, the authors suggest that in principle, there's no reason it couldn't also be trained with reinforcement learning.

However, as previously discussed, there is a limitation in how much context Gato can process at once, referred to as context length. Context length represents the number of tokens (pieces of information) that the model can pay attention to at any given time. If the context length is too short, Gato might not have enough information to properly understand and respond to complex tasks, especially those that change over time (which would be represented as multiple 'timesteps' in the environment).

In conclusion, Gato represents a significant step forward in the development of AGI systems that can operate effectively across a wide range of tasks and domains. However, it should be noted that while it's a promising development, it's still a research project, and as with any AI system, it's likely to have limitations and areas where further refinement and training will be required.

Risks

Generalist agents, like Gato, could inadvertently create unwanted outcomes through cross-domain knowledge transfer and could pose safety and ethical concerns.

Generalist systems could also have unintended societal impacts due to unforeseen situations or insufficient oversight, stressing the importance of careful design and deployment. In addition, better understanding of these models requires extensive experimentation.

Domain Specific Models

It is likely that we will see the emergence of domain-specific transformer models in the coming years. These are adaptations of transformer models such as GPT (Generative Pretrained Transformer), which are specifically trained to perform tasks within a certain domain or field of knowledge.

The advantage of these domain-specific models is that they can provide more accurate, relevant, and knowledgeable responses in their areas of expertise. This is because the datasets used for their training are selected or created to reflect the specific knowledge and language of the domain, and the models are fine-tuned to perform tasks that are commonly needed in that domain.

Here is a few potential examples:

- **DoctorGPT**: A model like DoctorGPT could be trained on a dataset of medical textbooks, research papers, case studies, and patient-doctor conversations. Its use could range from assisting doctors in diagnosing diseases based on symptoms to providing laypeople with general medical advice. However, it's important to note that such an AI system should not replace professional medical advice and supervision.
- **LawyerGPT**: Similarly, LawyerGPT could be trained on a dataset consisting of legal texts, case law, contracts, and legal opinions. It could

assist in tasks such as drafting legal documents, providing legal information, or helping to identify relevant precedents for a particular case. Again, while it can support legal professionals, it would not replace the need for a human lawyer, particularly given the complexities and ethical considerations inherent in legal work.

These domain-specific models can make AI applications more efficient and useful in specific fields. However, it's important to remember that while they can offer special-ized knowledge, they don't possess human qualities like intuition, empathy, professional judgment, and they are ultimately based on the data they were trained on, which may have its own limitations and biases.

———

Test Your Knowledge

A. What is a generalist AI agent?

1. An AI that is restricted to one specific task
2. An AI that excels in multiple tasks across various domains
3. An AI that can only understand text
4. An AI that can only understand images

B. What is Gato?

1. A new video game

2. A generalist AI model developed by Google's DeepMind
3. A type of programming language
4. A new social media platform

C. What does Gato use to handle different types of data inputs?

1. Encryption
2. Compression
3. Tokenization
4. Data segmentation

D. What is the limitation of Gato in processing context?

1. It can only process a limited number of tokens at once
2. It cannot process text
3. It cannot process images
4. It only processes data in one language

E. What are some potential risks of generalist agents like Gato?

1. They can't understand human languages
2. They can create unwanted outcomes and pose safety and ethical concerns
3. They have no risks
4. They can cause internet outages

F. What are domain-specific transformer models?

1. Models specifically trained to perform tasks within a certain domain
2. Models that transform data from one domain to another
3. Models that can only process data in a specific language
4. Models that specialize in transforming images into text

G. What is the advantage of domain-specific models like DoctorGPT and LawyerGPT?

1. They can provide more accurate and knowledgeable responses in their areas of expertise
2. They can replace human professionals entirely
3. They can understand any language
4. They have no advantages

H. What are some limitations and biases of domain-specific models?

1. They don't possess human qualities like intuition and empathy, and they're based on the data they were trained on
2. They can't understand text or images
3. They can only work in one specific domain
4. They can't interact with humans in any meaningful way

Test your knowledge online.

Chapter 43
Generative Adversarial Networks

Generative Adversarial Networks (GANs) are a type of neural network that can generate entirely new content. They consist of two parts: a generator network that creates new data, and a discriminator network that tries to distinguish the generated data from real data.

Imagine an art forger (the generator) trying to create a perfect copy of a famous painting and an art detective (the discriminator) trying to spot the forgery. The forger gets better as they learn from the detective's critiques, and the detective also improves as the forgeries become more convincing. This continuous feedback loop results in the creation of new content that's almost indistinguishable from the real thing.

Now, imagine this process automated and accelerated by AI - welcome to the world of GANs.

GANs are behind many of the impressive feats of AI you may have seen, such as creating photorealistic images of human faces, transforming sketches into color images, or even generating images from textual descriptions.

GANs are important because they have the potential to generate new data that can be almost indistinguishable from real data. This ability opens up a world of possibilities across numerous industries and fields.

Let's take a look at some practical applications of GANs that are relevant to businesses.

- **Retail and Fashion**: GANs can be used to generate images of various fashion items or accessories in different settings, helping customers visualize products in real-world scenarios. They can also assist designers in creating new fashion designs based on certain inputs or trends.
- **Real Estate**: GANs can take the blueprint of a house and generate images of how each room might look when furnished, providing potential buyers with a more immersive experience.
- **Entertainment and Media**: GANs can be used to generate new characters for video games or animated films based on a set of parameters, greatly reducing the time and cost of content creation.

- **Healthcare: GAN**s can generate medical images to aid in training and research without compromising patient privacy.

Test Your Knowledge

A. What are the two parts of a Generative Adversarial Network (GAN)?

1. The recognizer and the forgetter
2. The generator network and the discriminator network
3. The input neurons and the output neurons
4. The encoder and the decoder

B. What is a common application of GANs?

1. Predicting the price of a house
2. Creating photorealistic images of human faces
3. Understanding spoken language
4. Reading a book

Test your knowledge online.

Chapter 44
Diffusion Models

In the previous chapter we discussed GANs, a significant breakthrough in artificial intelligence capable of generating near-realistic images. Now, we shift our focus to Diffusion Models, which promises potential advancements in the field of image generation.

Let's start by drawing an analogy. If you've ever mixed sugar in your coffee, you've witnessed diffusion - a process where particles (sugar) move from an area of high concentration to one of lower concentration until they are evenly dispersed. This concept of diffusion, when transposed into the realm of AI, forms the basis of diffusion models.

Diffusion models, in essence, are generative models that gradually introduce or eliminate 'noise' to generate data samples, such as images. They start with an image (the data) and introduce noise, distorting the original image. Then, through a process of reversing the steps, the noise is removed to recreate an image - possibly an entirely new one.

Let's bring in an example to illustrate this better. Consider a clothing company planning to launch a new collection of t-shirts. They would like to generate various design options. With a Diffusion Model, they can create multiple, unique designs by starting from a noise image. This can be done either unconditionally, akin to asking the model for a random design, or conditionally, by providing specific instructions, such as a t-shirt featuring a sunset and palm trees.

These days, we can even use diffusion models to generate videos from text prompts.

The next question that arises is - how do diffusion models compare to GANs? While both generate images, the methods they employ are fundamentally different. As previously discussed, a GAN comprises two models, the generator and the discriminator. These models engage in a continuous game, with the generator trying to create images and the discriminator determining their authenticity. The process continues until the generator creates images so convincingly that the discriminator cannot differentiate between the real and generated images.

In contrast, diffusion models don't involve such competition. They follow a method similar to the diffusion process described earlier. A key benefit of this approach is that unlike the competitive mechanism of GANs, which can be hard to balance, diffusion models tend to be more stable during training, and their single-model structure simplifies handling.

However, it is important to mention that diffusion models are not without their limitations. For instance, the process of introducing and eliminating noise happens over several iterations, which can be time-consuming. That said, recent progress in this field has led to methods that minimize the required steps, thereby speeding up the process.

Some well-known diffusion models for image generation include Dall-E 2 by OpenAI, Imagen by Google, Stable Diffusion by StabilityAI, Kaiber, and Midjourney. These models have shown great promise in the generation of high-quality, detailed images based on input prompts and are continuing to evolve.

Diffusion models possess the potential to substantially enhance the realm of creativity and content generation as a whole. Their proficiency has already made significant strides in recent months and is evolving fast.

———

Test Your Knowledge

A. What is a Diffusion Model in the context of AI?

1. A model that diffuses information
2. A model that gradually introduces or eliminates 'noise' to generate data samples

3. A model that generates noise
4. A model that reduces noise in data

B. How does a Diffusion Model generate images?

1. It starts with a noise image and introduces more noise
2. It starts with an image, introduces noise, and then removes the noise to recreate an image
3. It starts with an image and adds more images to it
4. It starts with a noise image and removes noise to create an image

C. How do Diffusion Models compare to GANs?

1. Both are exactly the same
2. Both generate images, but their methods are fundamentally different
3. Both generate images using noise
4. Both use a generator and a discriminator model

D. What is a limitation of Diffusion Models?

1. They can't generate images
2. They can't eliminate noise
3. They require several iterations to introduce and eliminate noise, which can be time-consuming
4. They are too complex to use

E. What potential do Diffusion Models have in the realm of creativity and content generation?

1. They can enhance the quality of content
2. They can create new types of content
3. They can replace human creativity
4. They can substantially enhance the realm of creativity and content generation

F. How are Diffusion Models evolving?

1. They are becoming slower
2. They are becoming less stable
3. They are reducing in number
4. They are making significant strides in image generation and evolving quickly

Test your knowledge online.

Chapter 45
Foundation Models

Foundation models represent a significant shift in the field of artificial intelligence, transforming the landscape from narrowly defined, task-specific models to flexible and reusable AI systems. Coined by the Stanford Institute for Human-Centered Artificial Intelligence (HAI), the term "Foundation Models" signifies the advent of models that can be utilized across various domains and industry tasks.

Though the creation of these models is a resource-intensive process, requiring substantial computational power and extensive data sets, their potential applicability and scalability make them a worthy investment. They are designed to process massive amounts of data, exemplified by models such as ChatGPT and Midjourney that have been trained on ten thousand NVIDIA GPUs. The result is AI models with hundreds of billions of hyperparameters that allow them to adapt and respond to an unlimited number of tasks.

Models like GPT-4 and BERT are not confined to a specific task but can generate text or learn from one situation and apply it to another, respectively, marking a level of versatility akin to human cognitive abilities. Foundation models can extrapolate from broad sets of unlabeled data, exhibiting a kind of AI 'creativity' that can be harnessed for a variety of purposes, from writing poetry to summarizing lengthy documents.

One of the greatest advantages of foundation models is their potential to reduce the labor-intensive data labeling process significantly. This ability is particularly beneficial in areas such as natural language processing, where foundation models can be fine-tuned on a domain-specific unlabeled corpus and a smaller amount of labeled data, rather than requiring tens of thousands of labeled examples.

Beyond their obvious applications in language-related tasks, foundation models are proving transformative in fields as diverse as coding and financial services. They can automate business processes, generate images from text descriptions, or be tailored for specific tasks such as sentiment analysis.

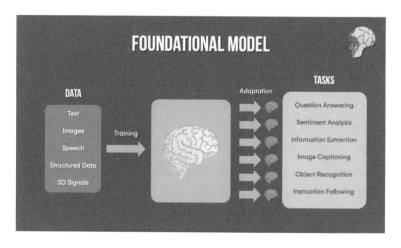

In conclusion, the advent of foundation models is a testament to the rapid advancements in artificial intelligence, marking a shift from task-specific models to versatile and reusable systems. Despite the significant resources required for their creation, their potential to automate a wide variety of tasks and reduce the dependency on labeled data is set to revolutionize industries. As these models continue to evolve, they will undoubtedly catalyze a new era of AI-driven innovation and productivity.

———

Test Your Knowledge

A. What distinguishes foundation models from the previous, task-specific AI models?

1. Foundation models require fewer resources to create.

2. Foundation models can only be used in the tech industry.
3. Foundation models are trained on broad sets of unlabeled data and can be applied to a significant number of tasks.
4. Foundation models are not capable of 'creativity.'

B. What is one of the main advantages of foundation models in natural language processing?

1. They increase the amount of labeled data required.
2. They can reduce the labor-intensive data labeling process significantly.
3. They cannot generate text.
4. They can only be used for sentiment analysis.

C. The advent of foundation models marks a shift from _____ to _____.

1. Costly models; inexpensive models.
2. Task-specific models; versatile and reusable systems.
3. Unlabeled data; labeled data.
4. Resource-intensive models; resource-light models.

E. Despite the significant resources required for their creation, why are foundation models considered a worthy investment?

1. They can perform only a single task.
2. They are not reusable.
3. They have the potential to automate a wide variety of tasks and reduce dependency on labeled data.
4. They require substantial computational power to run.

Test your knowledge online here.

Chapter 46
The Generative AI Value Chain

The rise of Gen AI has led to a new value chain consisting of six key areas:

1. Hardware,
2. Cloud platforms,
3. Foundation models,
4. Model hubs and machine learning operations (MLOps),
5. Applications,
6. Services.

This has spurred an ecosystem of hardware providers and application builders, though the most significant value creation lies in building end-user applications.

Gen AI models are more complex than traditional AI systems, hence raising the barriers for new and small companies. Large tech giants currently dominate many areas of the value chain.

In the **hardware sector**, NVIDIA and Google lead the chip design market, with Taiwan Semiconductor Manufacturing Company Limited producing almost all accelerator chips. Given the high costs and specialized skills needed, it's challenging for new market entrants.

Cloud platforms are crucial as they allow businesses to build, tune, and run AI models without incurring the high costs of maintaining on-premises hardware. Major cloud providers offer comprehensive platforms for running Gen AI workloads.

Foundation models, central to Gen AI, are pretrained to create specific types of content and can be adapted for various tasks. As discussed previously, developing these models demands significant resources, expertise, and money, making this area largely dominated by tech giants and heavily funded startups. However, some startups like Cohere, Anthropic, and AI21 have had success in developing their own large language models.

Model hubs and MLOps are required for businesses to store and access foundation models and adapt them for end-user applications. Depending on whether the models are closed-source or open-source, the developer of the foundation model or independent model hubs provide these services.

The **applications** built on top of foundation models enable specific tasks, such as customer service or drafting marketing emails. The highest value creation potential lies in applications that leverage fine-tuned foundation models, customized for a particular use case. Developers might use proprietary data, feedback loops, or deep industry knowledge to fine-tune these models.

Gen AI is expected to have significant impact on various business functions and industries. IT, marketing and sales, customer service, and product development are anticipated to be most affected in the first wave of applications. Industries such as media and entertainment, life sciences, banking, consumer, telecommunications, and technology can experience significant operational efficiencies due to their substantial investments in these functions.

Generative AI services will emerge to help businesses navigate the complexities and opportunities of this technology. Existing AI service providers are likely to evolve their offerings to cater to this market, with niche players also entering the field with specialized knowledge.

In conclusion, while Gen AI and its supporting ecosystem are still developing, applications built on fine-tuned foundation models offer the most substantial value-creation opportunities.

———

Test Your Knowledge

A. What is the main role of cloud platforms in the context of generative AI?

1. They allow businesses to develop AI hardware.
2. They enable businesses to build, tune, and run AI models without the high cost of maintaining on-premises hardware.
3. They assist businesses in creating open-source AI models.
4. They help businesses market their AI applications.

B. In the generative AI value chain, where does the most significant value creation lie?

1. In the hardware sector
2. In cloud platforms
3. In foundation models
4. In building end-user applications

C. How can developers enhance the effectiveness of applications built on top of foundation models?

1. By using proprietary data, feedback loops, or deep industry knowledge to fine-tune these models.
2. By increasing the size of the foundation models.
3. By converting the models to open-source.
4. By relying solely on pre-training data.

Test your knowledge online here.

Chapter 47
Training GPT Assistants and the Art of Prompting

In the evolving sphere of artificial intelligence, Generative Pretrained Transformer models, like the powerful GPT-4, have emerged as groundbreaking tools that have revolutionized the approach to language-based tasks.

Now we will explore the intricate process of training these Large Language Models (LLMs), along with a profound focus on the art of prompting. We'll underscore the critical role of careful fine-tuning, the strengths and limitations of these AI assistants, and the importance of crafting precise prompts for optimal results.

Training GPT Assistants: The Process

Training a GPT model involves an intricate, multi-layered process that requires substantial technical expertise. The initial step, is pretraining. This involves training a model on a large corpus of internet text, enabling the model to learn the statistical structure of the language. The GPT-4 model, for instance, is pretrained on an expansive array of documents, including books, articles, and websites.

The pretraining phase gives the model a powerful base, but it is through fine-tuning that the model becomes a specialized assistant. Fine-tuning is a subsequent phase where the pretrained model is further trained on a specific dataset, targeting a particular task or application. It is during this phase that the model is taught to generate desired outputs for given inputs or prompts.

However, fine-tuning is a complex and technically demanding task. It requires specialized data sets, often created by human data contractors, or advanced synthetic data pipelines. Moreover, the fine-tuning process slows down the iteration cycle significantly due to its intricate nature.

Supervised Fine-Tuning and Reinforcement Learning from Human Feedback

OpenAI currently uses two types of fine-tuning processes: Supervised Fine Tuning (SFT) and Reinforcement Learning from Human Feedback (RLHF). SFT involves the continuation of the language modelling task, making it a more straightforward method. In contrast, RLHF is a cutting-edge research area involving the use of feedback to improve the model's performance.

While RLHF might offer better results than SFT if executed correctly, Karpathy from OpenAI warns against rushing into it without sufficient expertise as it is a domain that is difficult to navigate, unstable, and evolving fast.

The Power of Prompts

The potential of an LLM hinges not just on its training but significantly on how it is prompted or asked questions. The crafting of prompts requires precision, relevant context, and an understanding of how the LLM reasons.

Prompts, in essence, are detailed instructions that guide the LLM. They should be informative, presenting relevant context, and detailed enough for the model to understand the task at hand. We can think of an LLM as a colleague who is being asked to perform a task and cannot ask clarifying questions. Thus, the prompts must be clear and unambiguous.

Harnessing the Art of Prompt Engineering

Crafting highly effective prompts involves not only detailed task instructions but also incorporating short examples wherever possible, essentially showing rather than just telling. This approach helps the LLM better grasp the nature of the task, thus enhancing its performance.

Prompt engineering also extends beyond individual tasks. We should think about the continuity of prompts and responses, considering how they could be glued together, and the potential of generating multiple samples.

We will provide prompt strategies in the next chapter.

Taking Performance to the Next Level: Fine-tuning

Fine-tuning the model is the next step once you've mastered the art of prompting. This is the slow and highly involved method of adjusting the model's parameters for a specific application.

GPT Assistants: Applications and Limitations

There are both opportunities and challenges in utilizing LLMs. They are well-suited for low-stakes applications, where their potential errors or biases would have limited impact. Always combining them with human oversight is crucial due to their current limitations such as possible biases, tendency to fabricate information, reasoning errors, and knowledge cutoffs. They are also susceptible to various forms of attacks such as prompt injection, jailbreak attacks, and data poisoning attacks.

- **Prompt Injection**: Refer to an attack where an adversary manipulates the input prompt to an AI model in order to influence or control its output. For instance, an attacker might carefully craft a prompt that seems innocuous but leads the AI to generate harmful or misleading content. This could be used to spread disinformation, propagate harmful biases, or exploit other vulnerabilities in the model's behavior.

- **Jailbreak Attacks**: "Jailbreaking" refers to bypassing the limitations or restrictions that have been placed on a system. In the context of AI, a "jailbreak attack" could involve finding ways to get an AI system to behave in ways that its developers didn't intend or anticipate, effectively "breaking out" of the "jail" of its intended operational parameters. For example, if an AI has been designed to refuse to generate certain kinds of content, a jailbreak attack might find a way around these safeguards.

- **Data Poisoning Attacks**: A data poisoning attack involves introducing malicious data into the training set used to train an AI, with the aim of causing the model to learn incorrect patterns or behave in harmful ways. For instance, an attacker might introduce biased data to make the AI discriminate against certain groups, or misleading data to make the AI generate false information.

Looking Forward: The Evolving Landscape of LLMs

These models are intricate artifacts of knowledge and can handle tasks in a wide array of areas, from mathematics to coding. A vibrant ecosystem is being built around these models, with new tools and techniques constantly being developed.

In conclusion, the training of GPT assistants and crafting of efficient prompts are both a science and an art. It requires a blend of technical skills, a deep understanding of the models' workings, and a creative touch in prompting to harness the full potential of these AI tools.

Chapter 48
Prompt Strategies

The prompt is instrumental in steering many of the foundation models' response. In this chapter, we provide a few high-level strategies that guide a model's output. These are:

1. Completion
2. Instruction
3. Demonstration

Completion

Until recently, LLMs focused mainly on completion. Trained on extensive datasets, typically derived from diverse internet sources, these models would rely on their predictive capabilities to complete a given text based on the likelihood derived from their training data.

For instance, if you feed a basic LLM with the line "Twinkle twinkle little star," the model might continue with "how I wonder what you are," based on the probability of this continuation in its training data.

However, when asked for factual responses, such as "Who invented the telephone?", the basic model may generate a variety of responses, like "What are other inventions of the 19th century?"— largely influenced by the diverse context in its training data where search users may have followed the first question with a number of other questions.

To guide a completion model, you can start a pattern or sentence you would like the model to continue. This method, though effective, requires careful handling as it can generate inaccurate results. Moreover, these models might not discern where to end the generated text.

Instruction

Recently, the emphasis has shifted towards instruction-tuned LLMs, which prove to be more user-friendly, safer, and better aligned with user intent.

Instruction-tuned LLMs excel at executing specific prompts. They can be seen as advanced assistants, capable of understanding and accurately responding to your requests.

For example, if you ask "Who invented the telephone?", an instruction-tuned LLM is more likely to answer, "Alexander Graham Bell". This efficiency comes from a fine-tuning process that includes instruction-based inputs and outputs and further refinements through techniques like Reinforcement Learning from Human Feedback (RLHF). This process makes these LLMs more helpful, less prone to generating harmful or misleading content, and more reliable.

Demonstration

Finally, demonstration prompts, also known as few-shot learning, guide the model by offering examples. By giving the model a few specific examples in the prompt, it learns to generate the required output.

Here's an example of a demonstration prompt:

Quote: "Grown-ups love figures... When you tell them you've made a new friend they never ask you any questions about essential matters. They never say to you 'What does his voice sound like? What games does he love best? Does he collect butterflies?' Instead they demand 'How old is he? How much does he weigh? How much money does his father make?' Only from these figures do they think they have learned anything about him." — Antoine de Saint-Exupéry, The Little Prince

Author: Antoine de Saint-Exupéry

If a second quote is given without the author:

```
Quote: "Hope is the thing with feathers
that perches in the soul - and sings the
tunes without the words - and never stops
at all." — Emily Dickinson, Complete
Poems

Author:
```

The model, recognizing the format, would complete with:

```
Emily Dickinson
```

Best Practices for Using Instruction-tuned LLMs

Now we cover five key practices that will get you better results from LLMs.

1. Be clear and specific
2. Use delimiters to indicate distinct parts
3. Request a structured output
4. Ensure conditions are checked
5. Provide examples

1. Be Clear and Specific

Using LLMs optimally often hinges on the clarity and specificity of the instructions provided. Much like explaining a task to a well-educated, albeit unfamiliar, colleague, your instructions need to be detailed and unambiguous.

For instance, if you were to instruct, "Write an essay on Alexander Graham Bell," the generated output could cover a variety of topics, from Bell's personal life to his inventions. However, if you refine your request to, "Write an essay on the impact of Alexander Graham Bell's invention of the telephone on modern communication in a formal academic style," you provide the LLM with explicit instructions about the topic, focus, and tone. As a result, it's more likely to generate a response that meets your expectations.

2. Use Delimiters to Indicate Distinct Parts

Consider an instance where you want a one-line summary from a long paragraph. In this scenario, it could be beneficial to use distinct delimiters to clearly mark the paragraph in question. For example, you could enclose the text within square brackets [text]. Different punctuation marks, quotes, XML tags, or section titles can be employed as delimiters to distinctly separate parts of the text.

3. Request a Structured Output

Leveraging the model's ability to structure its output in a specific format can greatly facilitate subsequent processing or user interaction.

When you request information from a language model, especially in bulk or for a series of items, receiving it in a disorganized or free-flowing paragraph can make it hard to distinguish or process the individual pieces of information. However, if you provide a structure for the model to fill in, it can simplify the information presentation and make it easier to extract and utilize the specific data you need.

Suppose you want the model to generate a list of three fictitious symphony titles and their composers.

Symphony 1:

Composer 1:

Symphony 2:

Composer 2:

Symphony 3:

Composer 3:

The model's output will be easier to read and interpret. For instance, the model could respond:

Symphony 1: The Silent Dawn

Composer 1: Johann Amadeus Beethoven

Symphony 2: Ode to the Evening Star

Composer 2: Wilhelm Mozart Jr.

Symphony 3: Dance of the Autumn Leaves

Composer 3: Francisca Schubert

This organized output streamlines subsequent interactions with the data. It could also be easily converted into other formats, such as a spreadsheet or database, if needed for further analysis or use. It's a way of harnessing the model's flexibility to make your tasks easier.

4. Ensure Conditions are Checked

In scenarios where the task hinges on certain conditions, instruct the model to verify these conditions before proceeding with the task.

Suppose you want to extract certain financial information, such as revenue figures, from a company's annual report. However, not all annual reports follow the same format or include revenue data in the same way. Therefore, you would need to instruct the model to first verify that the necessary data is present in the text before proceeding.

Here's how you might frame your instruction: "If the annual report text provided contains specific revenue figures, extract and present this information. If the required data isn't present or unclear in the text, indicate that the data is unavailable or needs further clarification."

By instructing the model to verify the presence of the needed data before proceeding, you can ensure more accurate and useful output, avoiding potential misinterpretation of the text or inaccurate information extraction.

5. Provide Examples

Providing examples of successful completions (demonstration prompting) before asking the model to perform the actual task is another effective tactic. By providing a context and a style, the model can deliver results in a similar vein.

Let's consider a scenario where you want the model to translate English idioms into plain language.

```
Example 1:

Idiom: "Break a leg"

Plain Language: "Good luck"

Example 2:

Idiom: "Bite the bullet"

Plain Language: "Face a difficult situa-
tion bravely"
```

Now, you provide a new idiom:

```
Idiom: "Spill the beans"
```

Based on the previous examples, the model should output something similar to:

```
Plain Language: "Reveal a secret"
```

The demonstration prompting technique uses these example pairs to help guide the model's output. By providing these examples, the model has a better understanding of the task at hand.

In conclusion, getting the most out of a large language model requires a good understanding of the importance of the input prompt, a clear communication of your expectations, and the use of examples and structured prompts. By applying these strategies and tactics, you can interact more effectively with LLMs, and produce better outputs.

Moreover, the transformative potential of LLMs as a developer tool remains remarkably under-appreciated. Their capacity to leverage extensive training data and generate precise, contextual, and helpful information is a game-changer for the software development landscape. As a business leader, understanding the opportunities and limitation of LLMs will help you best guide your teams to great outcomes.

———

Test Your Knowledge

A. What is the purpose of a demonstration prompt?

1. It instructs the model to generate a specific type of output.
2. It guides the model by offering examples, helping it generate the required output.
3. It fine-tunes the model's response to fit a specific pattern.
4. It prompts the model to follow a set of instructions to generate the output.

B. When using large language models, why is it important to be clear and specific?

1. It helps in generating a more organized output.
2. It helps in instructing the model to verify certain conditions.
3. It helps in providing the model with explicit instructions about the topic, focus, and tone, making it more likely to generate a response that meets expectations.
4. It helps in providing examples for the model to follow.

C. Why is it important to request a structured output when interacting with a large language model?

1. It makes the output easier to read and interpret, and simplifies the information presentation.
2. It ensures the model checks for certain conditions before generating the output.
3. It guides the model by providing a set of rules to follow.
4. It enhances the clarity and specificity of the output.

D. In what scenario would it be important to instruct the model to check for certain conditions?

1. When you want to provide clear and specific instructions.
2. When you want to request a structured output.
3. When the task hinges on certain conditions, and the model needs to verify these conditions before proceeding with the task.

4. When you want to use delimiters to indicate distinct parts.

E. Why is it beneficial to provide examples when using large language models?

1. It helps in providing a structured output.
2. It helps in providing clear and specific instructions.
3. It helps in guiding the model's output, providing it with a better understanding of the task at hand.
4. It helps in instructing the model to check for certain conditions.

F. How can large language models transform the software development landscape?

1. By reducing the need for human intervention in the development process.
2. By leveraging extensive training data and generating precise, contextual, and helpful information.
3. By eliminating the need for traditional programming languages.
4. By making the development process completely automated.

Chapter 49

Regulating and Governing Generative AI: A Case Study of the European Union

As the power of AI grows, so too does the need for comprehensive regulations. In navigating the intricate ethical, legal, and societal issues of AI, the European Union (EU) is taking the helm, charting a course that countries worldwide can follow. This positions the EU as a compelling case study in AI regulation, providing invaluable insights for other jurisdictions.

The EU's proactive posture in building AI 'guardrails' reflects its understanding of the intrinsic risks and challenges tied to these complex technologies. With a focus on ethical dilemmas and privacy issues, the EU is dedicated to setting up a sturdy legal framework to mitigate potential AI-related harms while fostering technological innovation. The General Data Protection Regulation (GDPR) and the proposed Artificial Intelligence Act embody this commitment, encapsulating the EU's vision for a 'human-centric' AI ecosystem.

Meanwhile, the United States's approach to AI regulation remains distinct. While comprehensive AI-specific laws similar to the EU's framework are yet to be enacted, it doesn't signify a lawless AI environment. U.S. federal agencies, leveraging existing civil rights and consumer protection laws, have shown determination to take action against harmful AI products. Recent Senate hearings hint towards a growing awareness and an emerging willingness to further these regulatory efforts.

Currently, there is also no comprehensive national privacy regulation in place in the US. Instead, individual states have taken the initiative to pass their own privacy laws, with the California Consumer Privacy Act (CCPA) being the most stringent and comprehensive. While a comprehensive national privacy regulation is lacking, specific industries such as healthcare, education, and financial sectors have regulations in place to protect sensitive data within their respective domains. These industry-specific regulations aim to safeguard the privacy and security of personal information, ensuring that organizations operating in these sectors adhere to strict data protection practices.

The divergent paths of these two regulatory approaches shed light on the global conundrum of how to marry the potential of AI with its pitfalls. This chapter will delve into the complex task of governing Gen AI, consider the risks faced by downstream companies leveraging generative APIs, and outline potential mitigation strategies, all from the perspective of the EU's regulatory scenario.

The European Union's Artificial Intelligence Act and General Data Protection Regulation

The EU's Artificial Intelligence Act is an ambitious legal proposal released in 2021, aimed at harmonizing AI regulations across all EU member states. Modeled on a risk-based approach, it classifies AI systems into four categories, from 'Unacceptable risk' to 'Minimal risk', providing a comprehensive regulatory compass.

Mirroring the impact of the EU's General Data Protection Regulation (GDPR) that in 2018 became a global yardstick for data privacy, the EU AI Act is poised to shape worldwide standards.

The rapid evolution of Gen AI presents unique challenges for regulation, especially regarding data privacy and security. By focusing on the EU as a case study with its rigorous GDPR framework, we can glean insights into the management of these challenges.

The Complexities of 'Right to Erasure' in Generative AI

Gen AI models like GPT-4 don't retain specific training data, but instead, learn generalized patterns from the data. This raises critical questions about how to erase data from an AI model and whether it's even technically possible. Adding to this complexity, Gen AI models produce unique outputs for each prompt, making it difficult to predict or control their outputs consistently.

Legal Basis for Data Processing: Consent vs. Legitimate Interests

The legal basis for processing personal data presents a significant challenge in regulating Gen AI within the context of GDPR. Enforcement trends and forthcoming guidance from the European Data Protection Board (EDPB) suggest a shift towards 'consent' as the legal basis for processing data, putting greater responsibility on tech companies and demanding more transparency in data usage and protection.

Transparency and Proportionality in the Age of AI

The nature of Gen AI also poses challenges in terms of transparency and proportionality. Transparency is crucial for ensuring the rights of data subjects, but AI models' 'black box' nature obscures the internal workings of the system, leading to questions about trustworthiness and accountability.

In relation to proportionality, there's the challenge of deciding whether the benefits of using such AI models outweigh the potential risks to privacy and other rights. Balancing these competing interests is a complex task, as both have significant implications for individuals and society as a whole.

AI Governance and Enforcement in the EU

One of the primary challenges with the current regulation of AI is the issue of enforcement. The intricacies of AI technologies, along with their vast geographic reach, pose significant hurdles for regulatory bodies.

The EU, however, has taken noteworthy steps to ensure the effectiveness of their regulatory framework. Under the proposed AI Act, the European Commission will be responsible for market surveillance, aided by a network of national supervisory authorities. It also introduces hefty fines for non-compliance.

Nevertheless, the challenge of governance in AI is far from solved. There is an ongoing need for international cooperation, given the global nature of AI. Technological advancements are outpacing our ability to understand and regulate them, highlighting the urgency for harmonized regulatory frameworks across nations.

Moreover, given the democratized access to Gen AI, individual users and smaller entities also pose a governance challenge. Oversight mechanisms will need to strike a balance between ensuring compliance and promoting innovation.

The EU's Regulatory Approach: A Model for Other Jurisdictions?

The EU's approach to AI regulation, encapsulated by the AI Act and GDPR, has positioned it as a global leader in the regulation of emerging technologies. This 'precautionary' approach focuses on mitigating potential risks and harms before they occur. This contrasts with the 'reactive' approach seen in jurisdictions like the United States, where the emphasis is more on addressing problems after they have occurred.

While the EU's approach has its merits, it's not without its critics. Some argue that overregulation could stifle innovation and hinder the competitive positioning of EU companies in the global AI race. Others fear that the current regulations may not be adequate to handle future AI advancements.

Despite these concerns, the EU's regulatory framework offers valuable lessons for other jurisdictions considering their approach to AI regulation. These include the importance of a human-centric approach, a clear classification of AI risks, strong enforcement mechanisms, and a commitment to international cooperation.

Looking Ahead: Regulating Generative AI in the Future

As we look to the future, it's clear that the task of regulating Gen AI will continue to pose significant challenges. The rapid pace of technological change, combined with the global nature of AI, demands a dynamic and collaborative approach to regulation.

As with any new technology, there is a delicate balance to be struck between encouraging innovation and protecting against potential harms. Policy-makers must work closely with technologists, academics, industry leaders, and the public to ensure that regulation is informed, effective, and balanced.

A critical aspect of this is fostering greater transparency and understanding of AI. Policymakers must strive to demystify AI technologies, enabling a more informed public discourse around their regulation. They must also ensure that regulation is adaptable, capable of responding to future advancements in AI.

The journey to effective AI regulation is a complex one, fraught with challenges and uncertainties. However, with a commitment to dialogue, cooperation, and a human-centric approach, we can navigate this path successfully. The goal must always be to ensure that AI serves humanity responsibly and ethically, fostering a future where AI benefits are accessible and equitable, and its risks are well managed.

Risks and Challenges for Downstream Companies Leveraging Generative APIs

Downstream companies leveraging generative APIs, like OpenAI's GPT-4, grapple with numerous potential risks and challenges. Their utilization of these advanced AI models involves multifaceted issues, including data security, privacy, legal, ethical considerations, and business continuity risks. Recognizing and understanding these risks are vital for companies to effectively mitigate them while capitalizing on the advantages of these influential AI tools.

1. Data Security and Privacy

Gen AI models like GPT-4, trained on colossal volumes of data, may unintentionally memorize sensitive data points, despite the models' designed aim to generalize rather than memorize. This could lead to inadvertent disclosure of confidential information, which could infringe data privacy laws like the European Union's GDPR. Moreover, given the complexities of the "right to be forgotten" and the "right to rectification" under GDPR, companies must develop strategies to navigate these risks.

There is an ongoing ambiguity about how the "right to erasure" could be enforced with AI models. While data can be removed from a training set, it remains a technical challenge to extract that data from the model itself, considering the "hallucinatory" nature of AI models. The unpredictability and the potential for different "hallucinations" about the same data point add complexity to rectification and erasure issues.

2. Legal Liabilities

Gen AI presents significant legal liability risks. These models, capable of generating potentially harmful content, might infringe upon libel laws, copyright laws, or other legal norms, making the companies susceptible to potential lawsuits.

If an AI model produces content that damages a person's reputation—similar to a Google search—this could result in serious legal repercussions. Therefore, companies should implement robust content moderation and filtering mechanisms to avert these legal implications.

In particular, copyright infringement represents a significant legal liability risk for downstream companies. Since AI models are trained on vast datasets often scraped from the internet, there is a risk that they could inadvertently generate content that violates copyright laws. This poses a challenge in terms of transparency and proportionality. AI's 'black box' nature obscures the internal workings of the system, leading to trustworthiness and accountability issues.

The challenge of proportionality lies in deciding whether the benefits of using such AI models outweigh potential risks to privacy and other rights. Balancing these competing interests is a complicated task with significant implications for individuals and society as a whole.

3. Ethical Considerations

From an ethical perspective, Gen AI models also pose significant challenges. These models, while powerful, can unintentionally generate misleading, biased, or harmful content. Companies need to develop ethical guidelines for AI usage and put systems in place to quickly identify and rectify any such issues.

4. Business Continuity

The dependency on external APIs for crucial business functions introduces business continuity risks if the API provider experiences an outage, discontinues the service, or alters policies or pricing. Downstream companies need to have contingency plans in place and consider these risks when designing their systems.

Conclusion

To navigate these intricate risks, downstream companies need a comprehensive and proactive governance and risk management approach. This approach should include regular audits of data security practices, legal consultations to understand potential liabilities, ethical guidelines for AI use, and robust business continuity plans.

Moreover, staying informed about the evolving landscape of AI regulation and actively engaging in open dialogue with regulators, API providers, and other stakeholders is critical. Despite these challenges, the power and potential of Gen AI are significant. Through meticulous risk management, companies can harness the benefits of generative APIs, protect their interests, and maintain trust with their stakeholders.

Risk Mitigation Strategies

Companies active in developing or using AI must setup a strong internal governance, designate a lead AI ethics official and stand up an Ethics board. Here, best practices include:

1 Flexibility of Structure: Ethics boards can assume numerous forms, with most design choices being highly contextual, as there isn't a "one-size-fits-all" solution.

2 Additional Layer of Defense: Ethics boards should be considered as an extra safety net rather than an original entity in AI corporate governance. Their role largely aligns with, supports, or duplicates existing efforts, providing an extra layer of security in high-stakes scenarios, despite potential efficiency reductions.

3 Importance of Members: Merely establishing an ethics board is insufficient; the value derived largely depends on its members and their commitment and capability to fulfill its mission. Thus, careful appointment is critical, and poor choices can potentially jeopardize the board's existence.

4 Impact of Formalities: Some design choices may seem merely procedural (e.g., establishing quorum), but they can significantly influence the board's effectiveness (e.g., by impeding decision-making). Such choices shouldn't be overlooked.

Addressing the risks associated with Gen AI models requires a thorough understanding of these models and the potential issues they might cause. First and foremost, companies should ensure that their use of AI aligns with all relevant data protection and copyright laws. As part of this, companies should consider consulting with legal experts who can provide insight into potential liabilities and how to mitigate them.

Implementing robust data security measures is another essential step. This includes ensuring that the AI models don't inadvertently memorize sensitive information, as well as taking steps to safeguard any data used in the training process.

Beyond legal and security measures, companies must also develop and adhere to a set of ethical guidelines. These guidelines should outline how the AI models should be used, what types of content they should and shouldn't produce, and how any issues will be addressed should they arise. It's also essential to have systems in place to quickly identify and rectify any harmful content that is generated.

Finally, companies must plan for potential disruptions to their access to Gen APIs. This includes developing contingency plans to ensure business continuity in the event of an outage, service discontinuation, or changes to policies or pricing.

The Road Ahead

As AI continues to evolve, so too will the risks and challenges associated with its use. However, with a proactive approach and a commitment to ethical AI use, downstream companies can mitigate these risks and harness the potential of generative APIs.

The broader regulatory challenges surrounding Gen AI models, particularly within the comprehensive data protection framework of the EU, are complex. Nevertheless, by confronting these issues and encouraging dialogue between technologists, lawmakers, and wider society, we can shape a future where AI serves humanity responsibly and ethically.

While the regulatory journey may be fraught with hurdles, the destination—a harmonized framework that balances the benefits of AI with necessary protections—will be worth the effort. As AI technology advances and we become more aware of its implications, regulators and businesses must work together to ensure that the digital future is safe, inclusive, and beneficial for all.

Chapter 50

Assignment: AI Opportunities and Challenges for Business Leaders

Objective

To analyze the opportunities and challenges posed by the integration of Gen AI technologies in your business operations, and to design an initial strategic response to these insights.

Instructions

1 Identifying Opportunities: Analyze the potential opportunities offered by integrating Gen AI into your business model. Consider how leveraging Gen AI could enhance your business operations, improve efficiency, drive innovation, and create competitive advantage.

2 Assessing Challenges: Evaluate the challenges your business may face in implementing Gen AI technologies, particularly in relation to:

• Data Security and Privacy

• Legal Liabilities

• Ethical Considerations

• Business Continuity

3 Risk Mitigation: Outline potential strategies your business could implement to mitigate these challenges. This could include plans for data security, legal compliance, establishing ethical guidelines, and business continuity preparations. Consider best practices such as setting up an internal governance structure, appointing an AI ethics official, and setting up an Ethics board.

4 Regulatory Landscape: Analyze the current regulatory landscape in your jurisdiction, considering frameworks such as the EU's GDPR and AI Act. What are the implications of these regulations for your business, and how can you ensure compliance now and in the future?

5 Future Outlook: Finally, consider the future of AI in your business and industry. How might upcoming advancements or regulatory changes impact your operations? How can your business stay ahead of these changes and continue to innovate responsibly?

6 Presentation of Findings: Consolidate your findings into a report that presents your opportunity and challenge assessment, your proposed strategies for risk mitigation, and your outlook on future developments. This report should be written in a manner that can be understood by various stakeholders within your organization, including executives, managers, and technical staff.

Please remember to support your assessments and strategies with evidence, such as relevant industry examples, academic studies, and expert opinions.

Outcomes

A successful report will deliver an in-depth analysis, including the viability and thoroughness of key risk mitigation strategies, and a broad understanding of the future implications of AI on your business.

Use this report to demonstrate to key stakeholders a clear understanding of both the opportunities and challenges of AI, offering a strategic, forward-thinking approach to integrating AI responsibly and effectively into your business.

If you are enrolled in our course, you will receive feedback from the course instructor as part of the accreditation process.

You will also have an opportunity to validate and build on this report supported by upcoming books in our *Bytesized Learning* series.

We wish you success as you embark on your AI adoption journey.

Bye for now, and stay human!

END

Note: Consider leaving a review and sharing the book with others that may benefit from its content.

I encourage you to dive deeper into the technology powering generative AI by reviewing the books and courses on the next page.

Keep Learning

Our books

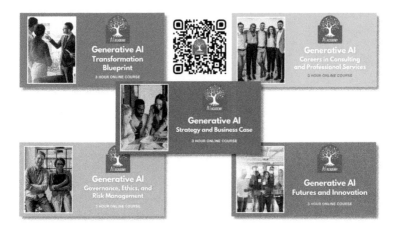

Our courses